Parents and Grandparents
as Spiritual Guides

~

Parents and Grandparents as Spiritual Guides

~

Nurturing Children of the Promise

by Betty Shannon Cloyd

UPPER ROOM BOOKS®
NASHVILLE

Parents and Grandparents as Spiritual Guides
Nurturing Children of the Promise
© 2000 by Betty Shannon Cloyd
All Rights Reserved.

The Upper Room® Website: http://www.upperroom.org

Appreciation is expressed to Joseph P. Horrigan, M.D., at the University of North Carolina for the interview and to all persons who granted permission to use their stories in this book.

Cover design: Gore Studio
Interior design: Nancy J. Cole
Cover photograph: © The Stock Market/Ariel Skelley
First printing: 2000

Library of Congress Cataloging-in-Publication Data

Cloyd, Betty Shannon.
    Parents and grandparents as spiritual guides: nurturing children of the promise / by Betty S. Cloyd.
        p. cm.
    Includes bibliographical references.
    ISBN 0-8358-0923-4
    1. Parenting-Religious aspects-Christianity. 2. Parents-Religious life. 3. Grandparents-Religious life. 4. Spiritual life-Christianity. I. Title.
    BV4529.C56 2000
    248.8'45—dc21   00-020803
                                                                          CIP

Printed in the United States of America

To my grandparents,
Pearl and Tom Cotton,
and my parents,
Lena Margaret and James Shannon,
who have each in special ways given me life,
physically and spiritually.

Most of all to Tom—encourager,
soul mate, and best friend—who
has always believed in me
and nudged me on to do far more than
I ever thought I could.

Contents

Acknowledgments   9

Introduction   11

Chapter One: The Promise Is for You   17

Chapter Two: All Life Is Holy, All Life Is One   35

Chapter Three: Letting God's Light Shine Through   53

Chapter Four: Grandparenting as a Gift   85

Chapter Five: Partners with God   107

Chapter Six: Our Life Together in God   135

Questions for Discussion   153

Notes   157

Bibliography   163

The Hannah Promise

The Lois Promise

Acknowledgments

In many ways writing a book is like having a baby—it causes a lot of flurry, especially at the end! Just as many people help with the birthing of a child, many people have come to my aid with their incredible encouragement, assistance, and wisdom. I am especially grateful to JoAnn Miller, executive editor of book publishing for Upper Room Books, for patiently guiding me throughout the entire process. Her help and timely insights have been invaluable. To Sarah Schaller-Linn for her assistance with research and other helpful deeds, I extend my heartfelt appreciation. My sincere thanks go to Karen F. Williams, my kind and attentive editor, for bringing this manuscript to its final rendition. Her diligent attention to form and detail is sincerely acknowledged. I am particularly grateful to the group of grandparents from First United Methodist Church, Springfield, Tennessee, who met with me several times, sharing their firsthand wisdom and knowledge about grandparenting. Their perceptive comments and nuggets of wisdom were priceless. Those persons who agreed to let me interview them have added so much to the integrity of the book, and I am indebted to each one of them. The words of Joseph P. Horrigan, M.D., have contributed so much to our understanding of children, and I am grateful for his generous spirit in sharing so much of his time and wisdom with me. I am exceedingly thankful for a special group of parents who were willing to become vulnerable by opening their hearts and sharing some of their painful experiences in parenting. Many readers will be blessed, I am sure, by their courageous stories. Some of the persons who have been in workshops or retreats that I have led have contributed to this book without even being aware of it! My thanks to all of you who read this book and find your stories within its pages. I am especially grateful to a group of persons who read the early drafts of my manuscripts and offered valuable suggestions and corrections. These include Pearl and C. H. Hunt, Dody Farmer, Carrie Malone, Marion Parr, and Suzanne Cloyd Hultman. Of course, it goes without saying that I could never have written this book without the constant encouragement and help of my husband, Tom. In the final days he became not only the cook and housekeeper but the midwife, proofreader, footnote specialist, and chief supporter and encourager. I am eternally grateful to him.

Introduction

For many years the focus of my life and ministry has been children. I have had the joy of rearing my own four children and now am happily participating in the lives of my grandchildren. Beyond this, I have had the great privilege of nurturing children from many walks of life through the ministry of Christian education. My husband and I have also had the unique opportunity of sharing in the lives of the children in The Democratic Republic of Congo, Africa, and among the children of the Navajo people in northern New Mexico. Children, then, have been and continue to be the joy of my life, as I am sure they are for many of you who read this book. Those of us who cherish children see them as "bearers of light" not only to us but also to the world around them and to the generations to come. They give our lives joy and meaning and, most of all, hope.

Even as I write these positive expressions about children, another part of me is filled with sadness. Scores of children in our midst are living with issues that no child should ever have to face, issues that threaten the very core of their innocence. These include fear, loneliness, neglect, abuse, abandonment, alienation, meaninglessness, and poverty of body and soul.

When I contrast my own relatively simple childhood with that of children today, I realize that today's world—especially the world of children—has changed dramatically since my early days in a small, rural town. During those days, children were—in part—reared by the whole community who embraced, nurtured, and accepted us. While our parents were the primary caregivers, the community was also deeply involved in the lives of its children. The adults with whom we were associated touched our lives in many ways as they taught us manners, corrected our grammar, instructed us how to live morally, and gave us words of encouragement and praise. They were well acquainted with our parents, and, more often than not, knew our grandparents, aunts, uncles and cousins as well!

Adults in those days had no fear of becoming involved in the lives of children. If children dared to disobey the well-defined code of behavior embraced by most of the people in our small town, the person who caught them transgressing reprimanded them. And the saga did not end there! The person who caught them was quick to inform their parents, and they were disciplined again at home. During those days, the inhabitants of any small town took seriously the task of being role model, mentor, and disciplinarian to the children in their midst.

At the same time that adult friends and neighbors were models of moral living and good citizenship, they were also spiritual guides for the children within the community. Persons who may have corrected our behavior during the week were the very same people we observed in our churches week after week. These were the persons we heard pray aloud during worship at church or before meals in the homes of our childhood friends.

For the most part, these were also the adults we observed daily, living out their faith by doing deeds of kindness and helping those in need. It was from these adults, as well as from our parents, that we learned what it meant to be a person of faith. We learned from them as we saw them provide food every day of the year for a young woman stricken with tuberculosis or for some other person in need in our community. We learned as we watched them care for the elderly in our midst, or as they taught our Sunday school classes weekly, or as they organized positive activities for the children of our community.

As children, we knew that these adults lived their faith day by day and we realized that this faith was a way of life for them and that it could be for us. We saw them as positive role models whom we could trust and follow, and we felt loved and cared for and protected by them. This sense of community, this sense of interconnection, gave our lives structure and meaning.

Our parents, then, did not bear the total burden of rearing their children or of nurturing them spiritually. There were always those nearby to help: friends, neighbors, and, more often than not, extended families. The community at-large, and society in general, also projected a positive force of reinforcement for the family and offered support for busy parents.

Today we are increasingly disconnected from one another and especially from the lives of children around us. We are fearful others will misunderstand our intentions toward children or perceive even our best motivations as something inappropriate. Our "Let's just not get involved" motto with regard to children creates a tragic break in relationships and diminishes our sense of community. Also, because of our mobile society, families often live hundreds of miles from their nearest relative. Frequently, parents find themselves living among persons who do not know their children and who do not choose to make an effort to get to know them. This, in itself, puts a great burden on parents. The isolation and loneliness that parents experience can be intensely devastating.

As a result, the lack of a community of caring people in the lives of children creates a tremendous crisis in the whole arena of family life. This void produces what authors David Hay and Rebecca Nye (*The Spirit of the Child*) call a "threadbare texture of community," which, in many parts of our society, impoverishes the spirit of numbers of children.

The effect of this loss of relationship is so great that children begin to lose touch with their spirituality.[1] The authors also say that when people lose intimate connections with others, there is "a rise of meaninglessness" that weakens moral consensus and causes social dislocations and crime.[2]

The breakdown of morals in our society is a great concern to the Christian community. The reality of evil is ever present, and increasingly we are made aware of crimes being committed in our cities, our small towns, and even in our own neighborhoods and often by persons who show no remorse. We learn of children committing crimes against one another and of being involved with drugs, alcohol, and guns, and we are fearful for our own safety and for the safety of our children. And we see signs of meaninglessness and despair in all levels of society.

Since this book is about children's spirituality, you might wonder why I am writing about the moral fiber of our country or of the crime and social dislocation that we see about us. The reason is simple. The morality of a society is directly related to the spirituality of the people. Evidence confirms that a person's "spirituality underpins ethical behavior and encourages social cohesion of a society."[3] After twenty years of research, Dr. David Hay, former director of the Religious Experience Research Centre in Oxford, England and director of the Children's Spirituality Project at the University of Nottingham, concludes that his most important single finding is the strong connection between spiritual awareness and ethical behavior. "Almost without exception," he says, "people link their spiritual or religious experience with a moral imperative."[4]

Hay and others conclude that spirituality has importance in maintaining the moral commonwealth and contributes to the coherence of society as a whole.[5] Spirituality makes persons look beyond themselves to the well-being of those around them. Their spirituality also makes persons more concerned about social justice and environmental issues.[6]

Amitai Etzioni, an American sociologist, has said that "what really matters is that by any measure the readings of social ill health are far too high for a civic society."[7] He continues with this admonition: "The best time to reinforce the moral and social foundations of institutions is not after they have collapsed but when they are cracking."[8] How we care for the spirituality of our children, then, is not only crucial for their own well-being; it is crucial for the well-being of our society as well.

The focus of this book is to urge parents, grandparents and other responsible adults in the home to reclaim the primary role of spiritual guide of their children in the context of the Christian faith. While it is true that children are born with a spirituality present in their life at birth, that spirituality must be protected, nurtured, and nourished if it is to grow. Just as we care for our children physically, emotionally, and mentally, we must care for them spiritually as well. This primary role cannot, must not, be neglected or relegated to some other person or agency. It is a role that those in the home must assume.

I hope this book will help you as the parent, grandparent, or someone who loves children see that to be the spiritual guide for your child is not an impossible task. You do not have to be a giant in the spiritual life to guide your children along this path; you must, however, be one who is intentionally seeking to go deeper in the life of the spirit. You must be a pilgrim on the journey toward God yourself.

This book provides practical guidelines on how to assume the role of spiritual guide to your child. Although I speak of parents and grandparents in this book, I mean to include anyone who is fulfilling the primary parental role in the child's life.

Specifically, the second chapter contains suggestions on how parents, grandparents, or others who have the primary care of children can have a more intentional spiritual life themselves. Chapter three gives specific ways that parents can be spiritual guides to their children, and chapter four is devoted to the grandparent's role as spiritual guide.

At the same time that I urge parents to be the primary spiritual guide for their children, I do not minimize the role of the church in this holy task. Parents must have the strong support, the resourcing and the encouragement of the church in this endeavor. I believe the family and the church should be in a sacred partnership, yoked together in this blessed privilege of providing children the spiritual foundation that they so desperately need. Parents and the community of faith should be devoted partners and allies, standing as a bulwark to protect children from the dangers and pitfalls of the world; standing as a bulwark to train, guide and nurture the spirit of their precious children.

I know that I cannot replicate the small communities of my childhood for those days are gone forever. However, I hope the community of faith can become what our small towns and villages once were: strong advocates for children and faithful partners with those who assume the primary role as spiritual guide. Adults in the community of faith must take seriously the vow that they make at every child's baptism to help raise that child in the way of Christ. They must reach out in warm hospitality to the children who are found both within and without the walls of the church, embracing them as if they were their own. The "threadbare texture of community" must be rewoven with the strong threads of love, support, protection and hope for the "least of these" in our midst. It takes the community of faith and the parent, undergirded by the power of the Holy Spirit, to form a child spiritually. Because our society is very bold about what it teaches our children today, all those who love children and assume responsibility for them have the obligation of being even bolder as we seek to nurture our children in the spiritual life.

If becoming a spiritual guide to your child seems like an overwhelming task to you, just remember that each journey in life begins with the first step. Someone has said that God cannot empower us for a pilgrimage until we say yes. So saying yes to this challenge is the first step. As you make a commitment to becoming a more spiritual person yourself and to being a spiritual guide for the special children in your midst, God's Holy Spirit will give you the strength and wisdom you need. It is a journey of faith, and you will find that just as you need it, step by step, day by day, and year by year, you will be enabled for the task. May God truly bless you as you embark on this exciting pilgrimage of faith!

Chapter One

─────

The Promise Is for You

Imagine for a moment that you are sitting in a room overlooking a small bay. The cloudless sky is vibrant blue and the scene tranquil and picturesque. Several small boats are in the harbor bobbing around as calmly as if they were toys in a bathtub. Suddenly, out of nowhere, a storm blows in and the boats, which were safe and peaceful a few moments ago, are thrown wildly about. The waves escalate until they are enormous, cascading over the little boats like giant waterfalls. It is evident that the small boats have become aimlessly adrift with little power to manage their own course. There is a question as to whether some of the fragile craft will even survive the storm.

Now turn your attention to a different place. Here you are seated at a window overlooking an exquisitely landscaped garden. In the center of the garden there is a small pond filled with lily pads, and instantly your attention is drawn to the intricate design created by the pads on the surface of the water. The picture is enhanced by colorful groupings of flowers and neatly manicured bushes and trees that surround the pond.

Again, as you are observing this peaceful scene, a storm suddenly arises. The rain falls in torrents and the wind sweeps the bushes and trees from side to side, threatening to uproot them. Finally, after the storm has continued for an hour or more, the rain and the wind subside, and you hurry outside to see what damage has been done to the beautiful garden. You notice that several small trees have, in fact, been uprooted, with leaves and debris scattered about. You anxiously run to the pond to see the damage there, and to your amazement you find that the lily pads maintain the exact design as before! Not one of them has been disturbed.

How can this possibly be, you wonder. It was such a violent storm. You find a stick and begin to poke around in the pond, and finally you think you have found the answer. You discover that the lily pads have an exceptional rootage system that extends deep into the soil below. This causes them to be anchored by a strong unobservable source far beneath the surface of the water. In addition, you find that the roots of each individual lily pad are intricately entwined with the roots of the other lily pads, giving them additional stability. These, then, you surmise, are the two factors that have enabled the lily pads to survive—a deep, secure root system that draws strength from being part of a larger intertwined system.

Why am I talking about boats in a harbor, lily pads on a pond and storms, you might wonder, when the focus of this book is on parents as spiritual guides for their children? The truth is that these two scenarios might well be the story of families today. When the winds blow and the rain comes, some families are like boats in the harbor with no anchor to hold them steady. Others are like the lily pads drawing strength from one another and from an unseen Source who gives them grounding and security in the storms of daily life.

Forces that Work against the Family

In our world, there are without a doubt many storms and forces—seen and unseen—pushing and pulling our families off course. With the existence of the drug culture, the pull of consumerism and materialism, the pressure of the electronic culture (TV, videos, computers, and movies), and a break-down of community and values, our children are faced with issues that did not impact families several decades ago. Recently a large group of mothers was asked to list their biggest challenge in parenting. Seventy-two percent of them stated that their greatest challenge was trying to control the effects of outside influences on their children.[1] These forces cannot be ignored.

In addition to the above mentioned forces that work against the family, another factor that greatly shapes today's family is the incredible mobility that is a part of our culture. Often families live hundreds of miles from their home of origin and from their closest relatives, causing the members to feel a deep sense of rootlessness, dislocation, loneliness, and alienation. It is unfortunate that in our world today, almost every force in society seems to work against the family instead of for it. These strong societal factors make it difficult for parents, grandparents, and significant adults in a child's life to hold their family steady in the storms of life.

How are families to survive amidst such strong outer forces? What can we do to give families the strength that they need to endure? The answer lies, I believe, in the family unit's ability to nurture and maintain a strong spiritual foundation or base, even in the midst of life's storms. Parents and grand-parents (or other loving adults in the home) are the pivotal persons in causing this to happen. In order to maintain a spiritual foundation, they must once again assume a strong role as spiritual guides for the children in their care.

For decades the home was seen as the primary center for Christian spiritual training. Parents, and other adults who assumed the role of spiritual guide for children, diligently taught them verses from the Bible and faithfully taught them how to pray. They were joined and strengthened in this endeavor by the community of faith and by the community at large. Thus the example and direction of adults helped instill children with integrity, character, Christian values, and virtues. That role has now changed, and many parents have begun to see the church as the primary center for issues dealing with the spiritual life. The role of the community has also changed as it has pulled away from the child and the parent, leaving an unfilled void. The church has done what it could, but it is becoming more and more apparent that in an hour or two a week the church cannot do all that is necessary in the spiritual formation of the child. Spiritual nurturing requires the diligent work of parents, grandparents, and other loving adults who will reclaim the role of spiritual guide for the children in their midst. Of course, it is essential that the parents be a part of a community of faith that can undergird them and provide nurture and nourishment for both the parents and the child in this endeavor.

A place to begin as we think about being spiritual guides is to understand that we are all spiritual beings, and as such, our spirituality must be nourished and nurtured. We are more than finite creatures who are put here on earth for a little while and then are gone. God has created us in God's image and claimed us to be God's own, and because of this, we differ from the rest of creation. We are more than flesh and blood; we are spiritual beings made for eternity.

Views of Life

Several years ago when my four children were small, I began to feel completely overwhelmed with my many child-rearing responsibilities. I often felt that I was performing one meaningless task after another. There was always too much to do and too little time to do it. The days somehow ran into one another, and I would find myself completing one chore only to repeat it the following day. It was during this time that I found a book that helped me tremendously. It was entitled *The Struggle of the Soul* by Lewis Joseph Sherrill.

In his book Sherrill describes three ways of looking at life. He says that one can view life as a treadmill, which evidently was the way I had begun to think about life. When one views life in this way, one lives life with a dismal feeling of meaninglessness and monotony. One day's activities are completed, only to be repeated again the following day, with no sense of achievement or joy.

Second, Sherrill says that it is possible to view life as a saga or epic. This saga tells our life story, with all its trials, suffering, and celebrations. The saga simply tells the human story of a particular time and in a particular place and is limited in the sense that it deals only with our human story.

Finally, one can view life as a pilgrimage. Sherrill states that there is a great difference in viewing life as a treadmill or saga and viewing life as a pilgrimage. Whereas life as a saga is lived only on the horizontal, human plane, life as a pilgrimage is lived on the vertical plane: that is, it is open to God and to eternity. Life as a pilgrimage is lived daily with God and in concert with God's presence and promises.[2] To view life in this manner gives life a refreshingly new outlook, because each day is filled with anticipation and hope. After reading this book, my attitude and my life took on a totally new meaning.

One thing more needs to be said about understanding life as a pilgrimage. We usually think of a pilgrim as someone who leaves the location in which they live to go to some faraway place in quest of some sacred person or thing. But Sherrill tells us that "pilgrimage is a state of mind before it is a journey, and many who deserve to be known as pilgrims can never take a journey of body. Yet they refuse to live in a treadmill."[3]

Few of us have the option of leaving our present location to go on a pilgrimage to some distant place. We have too many responsibilities and too many cherished relationships holding us where we are. Nonetheless, we can be pilgrims at heart while continuing to live where we are located, assuming all the duties and frustrations as before but living in the awareness of God's presence. When we do this, a change in our view of life is possible. We can begin to see life differently because we know now that we are on a sacred pilgrimage with God.

As we come to fully realize this truth, new options are open for us and all of life takes on a different meaning. Everything we do in the family now operates out of the underlying belief that we are on a pilgrimage together with God. This is our *modus operandi*. Of course, living life as a pilgrimage does not ensure that there will be no storms! Unfortunately, there will always be storms that threaten the family: storms of frustrations, disappointments, stress, financial issues, brokenness, separation, illness, and even death. Life will still at times resemble a treadmill. Occasionally life will still be seen as nothing more than a saga.

For the most part, however, when the wind blows and the rain pelts and the lightening strikes all around us, we are enabled to be calm in the midst of the storm because we know that God is with us. My younger daughter once gave me a plaque that I cherish. It says, "Sometimes God calms the storm; sometimes God lets the storm rage and calms His child." I have found this to be true in my life.

To acknowledge that God is with us and to teach our children to be attentive to God's daily presence gives the family the root system that is necessary to live with whatever events life brings us. Someone has said that before we can give our children wings, we have to give them roots! This is a good formula—roots first, then wings.

Who Are We?

My parents were strict with my three siblings and me. They held strong values consistent with those held by almost everyone in our small town. We were taught to be honest, kind, unselfish, caring, and respectful human beings. We were to obey adults, live the Golden Rule, and follow the Ten Commandments. There were no options. This is the way it was and to my knowledge we, as children, never questioned our parents about these values.

As my three siblings and I left home to go to a ball game or to some other activity, our parents always said to us, "Now while you are gone, remember who you are!" They did not have to elaborate on what they meant by that statement. We knew very well what they meant. "Don't forget all that we have taught you. Don't forget the rules that you are to live by." This was their underlying meaning.

In some respects, I gradually found this saying to be less than helpful. Although my parents had the best intention in saying it to us, the meaning became for me, "Don't forget to be who I want you to be or what I have taught you to be." Children sometimes build their identity on who they believe their parents want them to be, and this is not always helpful.

Some years ago, I was in a group where we were instructed to do an interesting exercise. We were each given a blank card and told to list three questions: Who are you? Who told you who you were? Who tells you who you are today? As we sought to answer these questions, those in the group began to sort out their feelings. Who are we really? Has someone from the past told us who we are? Are these voices still a dominant force in identifying who we are today? Some in the group identified themselves by their vocation. Some were teachers, professional church workers, homemakers, and so forth. Some of us identified ourselves by our relationships. We were wives, husbands, mothers, fathers, sisters, uncles.

However, some in the group realized their most important relationship and answered the question by saying they were children of God. This, of course, is the most important identity we have. This identity is the one that we long for and the one that gives our lives meaning and hope.

After I married and had four children, my husband and I changed the saying of my childhood. As our children left for various activities, we would say to them, "Don't forget *whose* you are." We felt that this was the important issue. We wanted our children to know that not only were they our children but God's as well. We wanted them to know that God loved them and claimed them.

In Isaiah 43:1-4, we read these consoling words:

> But now thus says the LORD,
> he who created you, O Jacob,
> he who formed you, O Israel:
> Do not fear, for I have redeemed you;
> I have called you by name, you are mine.
> When you pass through the waters,
>   I will be with you;
> and through the rivers, they
>   shall not overwhelm you;
> when you walk through fire you
>   shall not be burned,
> and the flame shall not
>   consume you.
> For I am the LORD your God,
> the Holy One of Israel, your Savior....
> Because you are precious in my sight,
> and honored, and I love you.

Today families desperately need the reassurance that they belong to God and are loved by God. Parents need reassurance that God is with them in their daily pilgrimage. Children, too, need to know that they are indeed precious in God's sight. Life is not always easy, and sometimes families are plunged into all kinds of rivers and fires through which they must walk. But the glorious thing is that we are all children of God and as spiritual beings, we are accompanied on this pilgrimage of life by. One who has created us, calls us by name, loves us infinitely, and promises to be with us always.

The Covenant Relationship

My grandfather, a devout man who lived his faith daily, greatly influenced my life. As a minister of the gospel, he served small churches for more than forty years. During his lifetime he acquired the reputation of being a peacemaker, and frequently, if a church had a problem, my grandfather was sent to resolve it. Somehow, in his quiet way, he was able to bring peace and unity where there had once been chaos.

Often my grandfather would gather his grandchildren around him for a time of prayer or for reading the scripture. He would take us in his arms and say to us, "Remember, now, you belong to God and God loves you very much." His words and actions always touched me deeply.

There are several different ways to describe our life together with God. My grandfather alluded to one of these ways. What he was saying, although he never used these words, was that we are in a covenant relationship with God. We belong to God, and because God loves us so much, we want to be in relationship with God. God has already chosen us to be God's people, and now we choose to accept that love and to live as God's own.

Another way of thinking of our life together with God is to say that because of God's promises to us, we make promises to God to live in a particular way, abiding by God's ways and God's commandments. We promise to live in the assurance of the presence and promises of God. However we choose to describe it, our life together with God is the important issue, no matter what words we use to describe this relationship. For it is in claiming this life with God that we find the strength and courage to face the demands that life brings us.

First, let us look briefly at the word *covenant*. One way to define covenant is to say that it is a holy agreement or set of promises between two parties. But when one of those parties is God, the covenant signifies a special relationship, a special connection. There are expectations in the covenant, but "there are also blessings and an amazing guarantee: Even when we fail, as we surely will since we are imperfect, God is ready to renew the covenant."[4]

Throughout the Bible, from Genesis to the Revelation of John, the concept of the covenant is present. Example after example exists of a loving God who is intent on bringing God's people into right relationship with God. Our response to the covenant, because of God's gracious initiative, is that we choose willingly to enter a binding agreement with God to walk daily with God and to follow God's ways.[5]

The Old Testament has several examples of covenant living. There is the story of Noah and the flood with God promising never again to destroy the world with water, and the rainbow is the sign of the covenant. There is also God's covenant with Abraham to make of Abraham's descendants a great nation. God's promise was fulfilled when a child was born to Abraham and Sarah in their old age, and from their descendants a great nation was born. And of course, the key covenant event between God and the Israelites was when God delivered them from Egyptian bondage and gave Moses the Ten Commandments. Jeremiah later summed up the meaning of covenant as "I will be your God, and you shall be my people" (Jer. 7:23; 31:33). We have this promise of God today.

When we turn to the New Testament, we find that Jesus came establishing a New Covenant between God and humankind through his sacrificial death on the cross. In this event, God was there claiming and loving God's people still, longing to be in divine relationship with humankind. Jesus was the fulfillment of the New Covenant.

In the biblical sense, covenant is most frequently thought of as the promise of God conditioned on certain terms on the part of humankind. In the covenant, God makes moral and ritual demands upon the people.[6] God has created us to be God's children, but if we are to be in covenant with God, we must meet the conditions set forth in the covenant. We can even choose to break the covenant we make with God and be disobedient. God, however, never breaks the covenant with us and continues always to be faithful to us, regardless of our actions.

Because God loves us with such an infinite love, we willingly enter into a covenant to be God's people. Claiming our place as beloved children of God and claiming the place of our children as beloved children of God are essential if we are to be all that God has created us to be. God says to us, "Claim your heritage. You are my people. You are loved by me and I promise to be with you. Now go and live in this love, keeping my commandments. Remember whose you are!"

Children of the Promise

Another way of thinking of our relationship with God is in using the word *promise*. A short verse tucked away in the fourth chapter of Paul's letter to the Galatians says, "Now you, my friends, are children of the promise..." (v. 28); and in Galatians 3:29 the writer refers to humankind as "heirs according to the promise." In Acts 2:39 we read, "For the promise is for you, for your children, and for all who are far away, everyone whom the Lord our God calls to him." These are the words for us to remember when we speak of our relationship with God: we are children of the promise. We are made in the image of God and are therefore spiritual beings rooted and grounded in Christ. And as such, we can claim our rightful place in the universe and begin to see life through a different set of lenses. We, as parents, are strengthened in our faith and are anchored in the power of God. From that stance, then, we are enabled to be spiritual guides for our children as they face the forces in society today.

Partners with God

Often our children's knowledge of and relationship with God startle us. We know that they are from God, yet they are wise in ways that often surprise us and catch us off guard. Ann Frances, who is now four, has always had an uncanny sense of the presence of God. From a very young age, she has been able to verbalize her feelings about that relationship. She speaks of God and Jesus often, in words that reflect a spiritual maturity advanced for her years.

Once when she was three, her mother was lying in the bed with her, trying to get her to go to sleep. At one point, Ann Frances became very excited and said, "Look, Mama, look, don't you see them? Don't you see them? There are God and Jesus right there above us, looking down on us."

On another occasion her mother was reading to Ann Frances. Since the book was not spiritual in any sense, her mother was surprised when Ann Frances interrupted the reading and said, "Mama, Mama, I just can't wait to go to heaven." Her mother replied, "Well, that's nice, Ann Frances, but we have to wait until God is ready for us," and then resumed reading. She thought about Ann Frances's statement and decided to pursue the subject more to see what Ann Frances had on her mind. "Why are you so excited and anxious to go to heaven, Ann Frances?" her mother asked. To which she replied, "So I can give God a big hug and kiss." As an afterthought she added, "And I want to see Nana and Gran" (her great-grandmothers).

There is a deep connection between the child and God. Someone has appropriately said, "God and children speak the same language." Their openness to the Spirit and God's love and concern for all children make our role as spiritual guide easier. We are in partnership with God in nurturing our children in the spiritual life.

Recently my younger son and his wife became the parents of a new son, whom they named Samuel. Samuel's birth came about after much prayer on their part and on the part of all of those who loved them. A child had been longed for and prayed for, but no child came. Tests were done and some problems discovered, and after much treatment a child was conceived. Needless to say, at the child's birth there was much thanksgiving! My son said that they chose to name the baby "Samuel" because they found in one translation that the name means "And God heard."

Their story reminds me of the story of Hannah in First Samuel. Hannah longed for a child and prayed often that God would bless her with an infant. She lived for years in that hope and expectation. The scripture says that the Lord remembered her, and in due time she conceived and bore a son. She named him Samuel because, she said, "I have asked him of the LORD" (1 Sam. 1:20).

In her time of longing, Hannah had promised God that if God would hear her prayer and give her a son, she would consecrate him to God. She would, at the proper time after weaning the child, place him in the temple with Eli and leave him there to do the Lord's work. After the baby arrived, how easy it would have been for Hannah to have forgotten her promise to the Lord! How easy it would have been to rationalize that Samuel needed her and she him. Instead Hannah was true to her promise, and at the proper time, she took Samuel to live with Eli in the temple.

She left him there with this saying: "So now I give him to the LORD. For his whole life he will be given over to the LORD" (1 Sam. 1:28, NIV). Hannah gives us a wonderful example of faithfulness to God. But more than that, she helps us see that our own children are gifts from God to us; they belonged to God before they were ours. Our partnership with God in guiding our children is a covenant relationship. We are recipients of the promise as we seek to nurture our children in the spiritual life. We realize that we cannot do it alone. The Holy Spirit will have to guide us day by day.

At first our inadequacy at being a spiritual guide to our children can threaten to overwhelm us. How can I possibly guide my child, we wonder; because to be a guide means to show the way by leading, or by directing, or by advising. Usually a guide becomes so because she or he has greater experience with the course to be pursued. This sometimes sends a shudder of fear through us. We know ourselves as parents to be so imperfect, so inadequate, so "unspiritual." We question if we are good enough, wise enough, experienced enough with things of the spirit to guide our children.

The truth is that one only has to be the spiritual guide one day at a time. That is much easier than thinking about a lifetime! You remember how God never left the children of Israel as they wandered in the desert. He met their needs daily by sending them food and water as they were needed. He sent a pillar of fire to guide them by night and pillar of cloud to cover them in the daytime. Just as God was faithful to the children of Israel, God will give us the strength we need daily as we guide our child in the spiritual life. In our own inadequacies, we come to know God as the Adequate One, for it is often in our weakness that God is able to be the strongest.

A Word as You Begin to Think about Being a Spiritual Guide

If you are the parent of young children, I would encourage you to practice the spiritual discipline of living in the present moment. Cherish each minute. Enjoy each smile. Relish each funny antic. Laugh often and love much. These days with your children are all too short. When older parents used to say those things to me when my children were small, I did not believe they could be true. How could these endless weary days and sleepless nights be too short! Now looking back, I know that my older, wiser friends were so right. Those days were, in fact, much, much too short.

Recently in re-reading one of my journals, I came across this entry that tells of my frequent inability to rejoice in the present moment: "I have been feeling a little melancholy lately, sensing deeply the loss of my parents in death, and the loneliness of having my children all away from home in various places. It is so strange that now that we have time to enjoy our parents, they are gone. The same is true of our children. Now that we have time for them, they are gone, out living their own lives—which is of course, what they should be doing! When they were all at home, though, we were always so busy. I believe that this makes a strong point that one should live every day to its fullest and relish each part of life. Will I ever learn this lesson or will it always come too late?"

The eighteenth-century French Jesuit, Jean-Pierre de Caussade, has a beautiful phrase for this ability to live with the awareness of the presence of God in each moment. He calls it the "sacrament of the present moment."

> God reveals himself to us through the most commonplace happenings in a way just as mysterious and just as truly and as worthy of adoration as in the great occurrences of history and the Scriptures.
>
> God speaks to every individual through what happens to them moment by moment.[7]

And so I would urge you to learn how to be present to the present moment. Spiritual guidance is actually about this one important thing—being present to the present moment and being present to the presence of God daily. It is about paying attention to the routine things, the things that do not seem to matter at the time. It is about being aware and listening each moment to what God is saying to us. This is not an easy lesson to learn and it takes time and discipline, but with God's help this must become a priority.

Often in our hectic family schedules, we are caught up in a "When-Then" mentality. "When the baby is out of diapers, then I will have time for prayers with the children." "When I have a better schedule at work, then I will work at this thing of spiritual nurture with the children." "When soccer season is over, then we will have time for family devotions."

Actually spiritual guidance takes place in the hectic midst of it all. It is a part of all the little things in life, the routine things, the things that do not seem to matter at the time. But do not be misled by the mundane in life. These day-to-day moments are hidden nuggets of opportunity for training our children in the things of the spirit. Do not let them pass you by.

Although we are intentional about what we hope to accomplish in the life of the child, we do not set up a schedule for "spiritual" moments. Spiritual nurture happens in the everyday activities during the pilgrimage through life with our children. From greeting them when they awaken in the morning to tucking them in bed at night, spiritual guidance occurs. This happens moment by moment, hour by hour, day by day, year by year throughout their childhood. We will look more in depth at some of the specifics of spiritual guidance in a later chapter.

The Spirituality of the Child

William Wordsworth says that children come from heaven "trailing clouds of glory," and those who have been around a newborn baby believe this to be true. We recently had a new granddaughter born into our family. One day as my husband carried our new granddaughter, this tiny pink bundle of love, he asked her, "Since you have just come from heaven, do you have a fresh word from God for us?" When I asked him what her reply was, he said, "Chloe said, 'I am the fresh word from God!'" Babies are indeed a "fresh word to us from God" and by their very being speak to us of all that is pure and innocent and holy.[8] We soon recognize that they have an uncanny knowledge of God and of things of the spirit. We are astounded that they have wisdom of spiritual things far beyond their years, and to our amazement it is wisdom that we have not taught them. There truly seems to be a mysterious bond between God and the child in our midst.

Because children are open to things of the spirit, this makes our role as spiritual guide easier. It is not so far back to God for the child as it is for us. Since our birth we, as adults, have taken on many other agendas, added many layers of baggage and become entangled in worldly matters and

COKESBURY BOOKSTORE
2907 CAPITOL AVE
SACRAMENTO   CA 95691

DATE: 01/26/01
MERH: 63105000071   TERH: 0002

S-A-L-E-S D-R-A-F-T

REF: 0973   BCH: 302
CD TYPE: MC
TR TYPE: PR
AMOUNT: $13.91

ACCT: 5424180303557604   EXP: 0302
AP: 144126
NAME: FRAN   ELDREDGE

I AGREE TO PAY ABOVE TOTAL AMOUNT
ACCORDING TO CARD ISSUER AGREEMENT
(MERCHANT AGREEMENT IF CREDIT VOUCHER)

X _____ 7. Eldredge _____
TOP COPY-MERCHANT BOTTOM COPY-CUSTOMER

...ts of faith that we
...racles and dubious

...o the mysteries of
...nises. Miracles are
...ot yet acquired the
...sical world. They
...t happen. They are
...ng Glass when she
...y as six impossible
...nbelievable seems

...nts today who say,
...faith tradition, and
...choose their own."
...or several reasons.
...ion in the spiritual
...the rootedness that
...an, it is natural to
...nt them formed in
...us. Second, if we
...basic personality of
...years than at any
...golden opportunity
...rd, we must realize
...spiritually, if not by
...will not remain a
...loose. The question

is, who do we want to assist them in this formation?

I believe we, as parents and grandparents, must take every opportunity to nurture our children spiritually by using the myriad of opportunities that are given to us in their childhood. And as we nurture them, we do it in the knowledge that we are not alone in the process. God, through the guidance of the Holy Spirit, will help us along the way, just as that help has come to Christians across the centuries. The spiritual guide is only God's vessel and must lead persons in God's way, not in his or her own way. The guide is used by God to open the path and to create space for the Holy Spirit to work. When we think of nurturing in this way, then we see ourselves as simply gateopeners for the Holy Spirit. Sofia Cavalletti says that "when we help the child to encounter God we are responding to the child's unspoken request: 'Help me to come close to God. Help me to be fully who I am.' "[9] We make time and space and then step aside so that the Holy Spirit can work in the life of the child that we cherish.

In the following chapters we will look more fully at what it means to be a spiritual guide.

Chapter Two

—

All Life Is Holy, All Life Is One

T he concept was not new to me, but somehow that day
the words struck a chord deep within. With fresh
insight I listened as some of our Native American
friends sang a beautiful song that included the words "All Life
Is Holy, All Life Is One." I knew that these words reflected
one of the tenants of Native American spirituality, that there
should be harmony in all of life. Hearing this song reminded
me anew of the ancient truth—that life is of one piece; it
cannot be splintered into segments.

As we live out our days, we cannot separate the secular
from the holy. One day is as sacred as another, and one task is
as blessed as the next when lived out in the presence of God.
What we do on Monday matters just as much as what we do
on Sunday. It is in the whole tapestry of life that we become
who we are, not in some isolated inspirational moment. The
spiritual life is formed in the middle of everyday life and by
everything that we do in life.

This is the first concept we need to understand as we
consider being a spiritual guide to our children—that all of
life is whole and holy. Our spirituality takes place in the rou-
tines of life—on the mountaintops and in the valleys, during
the mundane and the spectacular, as we clean house and as

we pray, as we drive carpools and as we visit the sick. In speaking with parents in various settings and on numerous occasions, I have often asked this question: "What is it that keeps your family from being the strong Christian family that you want it to be?" The answers are always interesting: lack of time for spiritual things—just too busy; outside influences and pressures; the electronic age (TV, computers, videos, VCRs, etc.); materialism and consumerism; conflicting values in society; lack of trust at all levels of society; the pervading self-centeredness of our culture; and parents' own insecurity with and sense of inadequacy in modeling the faith.

Joseph P. Horrigan, child psychiatrist and assistant professor in the Department of Psychiatry at the University of North Carolina at Chapel Hill, in a discussion about the issues that families face today, has some valuable insights. He contends that the increase of materialism in our culture today has created an avoidance of things of the spirit. He says that we often attempt to fill the spiritual void in our lives with "things"; and more often than not, these "things" are not very meaningful or satisfying. To buy and to have have become a means of filling the great emptiness that exists when we do not have the spiritual grounding for which our souls long.

Another issue Horrigan believes to be greatly impacting children is the fact that many of them are receiving inadequate supervision and lack quality time with their parents. He says this causes a feeling of emptiness in the lives of many children today.[1] Horrigan says that latchkey children, who come home day after day to an empty house and spend hours alone before their parents return from work, are a prime example. Judging from the children he sees, this phenomenon causes children to feel a deep sense of loneliness and alienation.

The difficulties of parenting are real in our world today. Some of the issues are easy to solve, others more difficult. For instance, while it is not in the parents' control to reverse the materialism of our culture, they can take steps to set guidelines for buying and spending in their family. Children can be taught values that are not centered in acquiring things. With regard to adequate quality time with children, because each family is different they must be creative in finding solutions to this issue. Since in many families both parents must work, the issue of adequate supervision and adequate quality time with children is a difficult one.

As I have talked with parents and grandparents about being spiritual guides to their children, their comments have been interesting. Some of the most frequently mentioned are:

"Well, I would like to do that, but I don't know how to do it very well."

"I wonder if it does any good anyway."

"Our children seem to be taking on the values of the culture and their peers."

"We just don't seem to have any influence any more."

Regardless of how prevalent the idea is that parents do not have any influence on their children, a study by Search Institute says differently. The study, seeking to find out what makes for effective faith maturity, included adolescents. The findings show that the two most powerful influences on faith maturity are the level of family religiousness and the amount of exposure to formal Christian education, such as Sunday school.[2] That is, the faith that is modeled and taught in the family and the lessons that are taught in formal Christian education settings are the two most powerful factors in producing a mature faith. What is this saying to us? It is saying that what takes place in our family does make a difference! It is saying that the family is a powerful unit for training and influencing the child in the spiritual life! While acknowledging the importance of the church in training their children in Christian education, families must boldly reclaim their vital role as the primary source of spiritual guidance for their children.

What Does the Term Spiritual Guide Mean?

Of course the word *spiritual* means of, or concerned with, or affecting the soul; or pertaining to God. Spirituality, then, describes the deep guiding force of our life shaped by our beliefs, practices, and relationship with God and others. Our spirituality is a response of our deepest self to God's spirit.

The term *spiritual guide*, on the other hand, may be new to you. What exactly does the term mean? What does a spiritual guide do for the child? We will consider these questions more fully in this chapter and later in chapter three.

In the history of Christianity, formal individual spiritual direction began in the third or fourth century. Persons desiring a deeper spiritual life sought out someone whom they felt was farther along on the spiritual journey. They met with them for guidance and prayer, usually on a regular basis and over a period of time. In the early centuries of the church, people walked for miles into the desert just to hear a word of advice or a word of hope from one of the desert fathers or mothers. (These were persons who retreated to the deserts of Egypt or Arabia to devote themselves to the life of prayer and meditation.) Not even the greatest saint would have attempted to go deeper in the spiritual life without the help of a spiritual guide. And I believe that if the greatest saints needed spiritual guides, how much more so do we.

There are many books available on spiritual direction, and from them we glean helpful definitions of the term *spiritual guide*. We will look at just a few of these.

Margaret Guenther says that spiritual directors or guides "are not professionals but are amateurs who aspire to reflect Christ's love."[3] She continues by saying that spiritual guidance involves "holy listening"—the listening to each other and ultimately to God.[4]

Kenneth Leech says that "the spiritual director (guide) exists to be a friend of the soul, a guide on the way to the City of God. [He/she] is not a leader but a guide, and he (she) points always beyond himself (herself) to the Kingdom and the Glory."[5]

And Sandra Schneiders says that "The guide is a companion in the...difficulties as well as in the joys of the spiritual life."[6]

I like the metaphor that one writer uses when he speaks of the spiritual guide as being only God's usher. "He/she is the means of God to open the path to the inward teaching of the Holy Spirit."[7]

A metaphor that I have used often is to speak of the parent or grandparent as being the "gateopener" for the Holy Spirit. We provide time and place and open the way for the Holy Spirit to enter the life of the child. That is, we offer hospitality for the Holy Spirit.[8] These metaphors, I believe, also accurately describe the work of the spiritual guide.

Gerald May, in *Care of Mind, Care of Spirit*, says that the " 'real' director or guide is the Holy Spirit, manifested though the relationship in a graced way."[9] And before we become too frightened at such a task or begin to feel that we are inadequate, May continues to assure us of our competency by saying that "lay people are as readily and legitimately called and gifted for this discipline [of being a spiritual guide] as are the ordained."[10] It is the Inner Guide, the Inner Teacher, who does the leading and teaching. We are just God's vessel or channel.

What do these definitions say to us about what the parent as spiritual guide does for the child? We will look at the answers to that question a little later, but first, let us look at one more necessary and vital component for being a spiritual guide. It is this: To be a spiritual guide for our children, we have to be on the journey ourselves. Tilden Edwards quotes Thomas Merton as saying that the effective spiritual guide is one "who knows that his or her first duty is to see to his (her) own interior life...since you never will be able to give to others what you do not possess yourself."[11] These words of Merton carry a strong message for parents and grandparents who want to be spiritual guides for their children. If we are serious about this task, we must be intentional about caring for our own spiritual lives, even as we are in the process of guiding our children along the way. There are many ways to do this, of course. The following are some solidly grounded spiritual disciplines used across the ages. These disciplines will enable us to open ourselves to God's presence and guidance so that God may shape and form us.

I. Be Attentive to God's Presence

We must develop an awareness of God's constant presence. We must be attentive to God, and we must teach our children to be attentive to God's presence. As we do this daily, we open a window to God and let God into our lives. We can be open to God's presence in many ways. For example, on awakening, begin each day with a verse of scripture or a short prayer of praise to God. The Psalms provide many verses that express praise and thanksgiving: "I will give thanks to the LORD with my whole heart; I will tell of all your wonderful deeds" (Ps. 9:1). "The LORD is my strength and my shield; in him my heart trusts" (Ps. 28:7).

We can also sing a song of faith as we awaken, such as "This is the day, this is the day, this is the day that the Lord has made." A wonderful African American choir that I am privileged to hear from time to time frequently sings the chorus, "God woke me up this morning and set me on my way." What a positive way to start the day with God! To affirm that God was with us when we awoke and that God has set us on our way gives hopeful direction for the day.

To close the day with praise to God puts a "bookend" around the day. Again we can use scripture. One of my favorites is "I will both lie down and sleep in peace; for you alone, O LORD, make me lie down in safety" (Ps. 4:8). Or, "Surely, goodness and mercy shall follow me all the days of my life, and I shall dwell in the house of the LORD for ever" (Ps. 23:6, KJV).

Another way to affirm God's presence is to use certain things or situations throughout the day to remind yourself that you are in God's presence. Examples of these might be the chiming of a clock, the ringing of a telephone, glancing at your watch, or stopping at traffic lights or stop signs. To realize that we are in the presence of God constantly gives us a sense of security and comfort.

All of life is lived in relationship with our loving God. We need to be attentive to this fact. John Wesley said that there are many things that "uncenter the soul from God." We need to find ways to keep our soul centered in the One who created us and is our constant companion.

2. Have a Daily Prayer Time

In order to have a deeper spiritual life, we must be diligent at having a daily time of prayer. Certainly we can pray anytime, anywhere, but having the discipline of a set time of prayer in a specific place is a great strength in our spiritual life. John Dalrymple says that in order to be able to pray all of the time everywhere, we must have prayed some of the time somewhere.[12] I would urge you to have a sacred space for yourself somewhere in your home. This might be a small table that represents an altar, a spot by your bed or by your favorite chair. This place can be for you a call to daily prayer.

Two other conditions essential for a vital prayer life are solitude and silence. I realize that if you are a parent, these are, perhaps, your two most precious commodities. I often remember how difficult it was to maintain my own prayer life when our four children were small. Sometimes my solitude and silence amounted to my running into the bathroom, closing the door, kneeling beside the tub for two minutes and praying, "Help, Lord!" But gradually with time and perseverance some solitude and silence opened for me, and it can for you too. Getting up thirty minutes earlier, or working out an agreement with your spouse or a friend to cover for you for thirty minutes a day, will allow you some solitude and silence. Staying up thirty minutes after the family has gone to bed might be a possibility for time alone in God's presence. You might want to use a combination of these ways to find time alone with God. God will help you find a way if you are serious about deepening your life of prayer.

3. Study the Scripture

The study of scripture is important as we seek to go deeper into our spiritual selves. We need to find ways to immerse ourselves in God's word, and there are several ways of doing this. I find it helpful to choose one book of the Bible and stay with that book as long as it seems productive. Read the words slowly, ruminating on them and letting God's message to you sink into your subconscious. If some of the verses touch you in a significant way, write them on a card and carry them with you as you go about your daily tasks. Refer to them frequently until they become imbedded in your memory.

An excellent way of reading the Bible called *lectio divina* or *divine reading* or *holy reading* has come down to us from the fourth century. As we read the Bible in this way we are not reading to gain information, nor are we reading to cover as much of the text as possible. We are, however, reading to discover what God is saying to us in the Holy Word; letting the words of the scripture form us spiritually. This form of reading the scripture uses Latin words for the four steps of lectio divina: *lectio*—read; *meditatio*—meditation; *oratio*—prayer, and *contemplatio*—contemplation.

In this four-step process, choose just a few verses of scripture and read them (*lectio*) slowly, prayerfully, and thoughtfully. Then spend a few minutes meditating (*meditatio*) on the passage trying to discern what word or phrase speaks to your heart and soul. What is God saying to you through the Word? In the third step, use the words or phrases that have touched you to form a prayer (*oratio*). That is, turn these enlivened words into a prayer and pray them back to God (*oratio*). In the final step, let the text sink from your mind to your heart (*contemplatio*) and rest in the blessing that it brings to you. In a prayerful mode, ask God to help you use this fresh Word in your daily life. By using this process, words that we have read and never noticed before can come alive for us as a life force taking control of our impulses and actions. It is a way of reading with an attitude of expectancy, a way of finding God's word for our individual lives.

Another strength that we find as we read the Bible is that we discover our own stories in the ancient stories of faith. Just as God showered steadfast love on these persons in the Bible so long ago, God also surrounds us with that same steadfast love. To realize that God is steadfast in our often unstable world brings us much strength and peace. To see that God forgave persons in the Bible who were not perfect and often stumbled along the way gives us hope and courage as we live out our lives.

Many years ago I remember reading that when the translators of one of the revisions of the Bible were trying to find the correct word for God's great, unconditional, ever-present love, they were having a difficult time finding such a word. Finally, one of the translators suggested "steadfast love." In one accord the other translators stood in agreement and began to sing the Doxology. When we read of God's steadfast love throughout the centuries, we too ought to stand and sing the Doxology!

Another excellent way to study the scripture and to grow in your prayer life is to use a prayer guide such as *A Guide to Prayer for All God's People*.[13] This resource includes a guide for a daily psalm, suggested scripture selections, various spiritual readings, and prayers. This helpful guide or another devotional book will provide a wonderful means for staying faithful to the discipline of Bible study.

4. Participate in a Small Group

If possible, be a part of a small group. This might be a prayer group that meets on a regular basis, a covenant group that holds each other accountable spiritually, or a group that uses some designated material for study. You might want to form a group composed of persons with children the ages of your children or grandchildren. That way you could share insights, compare your new understandings and learn from one another. (Do not, however, compare children.) There are many books available on how to begin a small group and to help you as you begin. If you do not find a group that meets your need already in existence, your pastor or someone on the staff of your church could help you organize one. There may also be others just waiting for such a group.

5. Journal Your Journey with God

Begin to journal as a spiritual discipline. The book that you use for journaling does not have to be anything fancy; just a spiral notebook will work well. Use your journal to record your inward journey and your communication with God. Also use your journal as a means of placing your children in God's presence, a way of seeking God's will as you guide your children day by day. You might also want to record an insight that has come to you either in your prayer time or in your study time.

Susan Shaughnessy says that not only is there value in the process of writing in our journals, it is also very helpful to review the content of journals at a later date. She feels that this can be a good resource for growth. She writes: "And there they [the journals] lie, waiting until a time when you revisit them and sift for gold."[14] As we reread our journals, we become amazed at how God has been faithful in our lives.

My oldest daughter Cindy helped me begin journaling years ago. Our family was going through a difficult time with illness. One day Cindy gave me a beautiful bound book as a gift. As I opened the book, I noticed the sheets were blank, and I looked at her questioningly. "I know you like to write," she said. "Why don't you try writing down some of your thoughts. That might help during this time." So I began and have been journaling, off and on now, for thirty years or more. Today as I opened one of my older journals and read several selections, I was overcome to read the words that I wrote years ago. To see that the issues that I was dealing with then have been resolved, often in miraculous ways, helps me comprehend that God's ongoing love and guidance surrounds me always. This, I believe, is one of the great benefits of journaling.

6. Use Fasting as a Spiritual Discipline

One of the least practiced, yet most rewarding, of the spiritual disciplines, is fasting for spiritual purposes. For a period of time, my husband and I chose to fast one day a week for a particular child in our family. Since we have four children, that worked well because in a month's time, we could fast for each one of them. In our day of fast foods, and all-you-can-eat food buffets, fasting is not a popular discipline; but it can be a great boost to your spiritual life.

I would like to suggest words of caution. Do not attempt a long fast before you have tried fasting for one meal. It is best to begin small and then increase the time that you fast. If you have any physical limitations at all, especially if you have diabetes, heart problems or are pregnant, seek your doctor's advice first. God does not require us to do those things that we are physically unable to do.

Richard Foster, in *Celebration of Discipline*, says do not try to run before you crawl, especially in fasting. He encourages beginning with a partial fast of twenty-four hours, for instance, lunch to lunch. This way, you are missing two meals, dinner and breakfast. With a partial fast, you may use fresh fruit juice and other liquids when you feel the need. After trying this type of fast two or three times, move to a twenty-four hour normal fast. In a normal fast you drink only water, but as much and as often as you like. After fasting in this manner on several occasions, you may want to move to a longer fast, perhaps a thirty-six hour fast, missing three meals.

With practice and focusing on the things of God, especially with regard to your children, you will be surprised at the blessings you will receive from fasting.

For those persons who cannot fast for medical reasons, other means of fasting are helpful. For example, if you watch television, fast from that and leave your television off for twenty-four hours. If you talk on the telephone, do not use your telephone for a period of time. We can also fast from negative thoughts and judgmental attitudes, striving to be more like Christ in all our thinking and actions. To deny ourselves of some pleasure for spiritual purposes enables us to center our minds and to hear more clearly God's message for our lives.

7. Retreat from the World Occasionally

Try to spend some time in a retreat setting away from the family at least once a quarter. (I would really like to suggest once a month, but I realize that this might be impossible with family schedules.) If you know of a retreat setting nearby, make reservations well in advance so that you can plan toward the date you select. If an overnight retreat is impossible, schedule a day retreat. If a whole day is impossible, schedule at least half a day.

If you do not know of a retreat setting, a quiet, unused room at your church is ideal. Perhaps you might be instrumental in establishing a retreat or meditation room at your church so that other parents and grandparents might use it as well. This would be a great service to others who might desire to use such a place. If you have a prayer chapel at your church, consider designating one day a week as a "retreat setting." This might encourage others to use it also.

We often take our values on how to act, what to believe, what car to drive, and what to wear from those around us. During our times of retreat, if we are serious about our spiritual life, we will learn to draw our strength from God, not from the world. This might take some practice on our part—

some withdrawal techniques. Perhaps "the world is too much with us," and we must now learn how to draw strength and receive guidance from God alone. Perhaps we have been trying to please the world or our neighbors or our relatives with our lifestyle. This time apart helps us reorder our lives.

In order to go on a retreat you must be intentional in planning this time apart. Plan for your spouse, a relative, or a friend to care for your children so that you can have some extended quiet time alone. Ideally, it would be good for you and your spouse to go together, but if this is not possible, then separate times will work.

During your time apart, and as God leads, spend some time considering a "master plan" or a "promise statement" for your family. If you truly consider yourself and your children to be children of the promise, what are some things that you will want to consider? Some questions to answer may be these: What do you really believe? What are your values? How will you pass them on to your family? What is God saying to you right now about your life and the lives of your children? An example of a promise statement to God follows:

> With God's help, I will have morning and evening prayers with my children. I will read or have them read, as appropriate, some part of the Bible every day.
>
> We will choose a verse every week as our "anchor verse," memorizing it, if possible, and using it in as many ways as possible. (Some ideas might be writing it on the family bulletin board or on small cards for each member to take with them, or posting it on mirrors.) I will look for ways to share my faith with my children, telling them of God's steadfast care.
>
> We will pray for others and do a good deed for someone every week. I, as father or mother, will maintain my own daily discipline of prayer and Bible study.
>
> Signed:
> Date:

Begin with only two or three of these promises, and then gradually add others as you feel God's leading. It is better to succeed in a few promises than to be overwhelmed with too many. Review this statement from time to time, revising it as God leads you.

In order to reevaluate what our priorities are and to reorder our lives, we need to spend time withdrawing from the world, literally if possible. And as we spend time in retreat and silence before God, praying and studying God's word, we begin to hear the voice of God saying silently in our hearts, "This is the way, walk in it. Lead your family in this direction."

8. Be Part of a Community of Faith

If you are to grow in your spiritual life, it is important for you and your children to be part of a vital community of faith. As our lives intersect with others who are growing in their faith, we gain strength for our own. Maintaining a strong spiritual life in isolation is difficult. When we share in the joys and sorrows of fellow pilgrims, we gain strength from one another.

In the first chapter, I told the story of the lily pads surviving a violent storm. They did this because of their deep root system and because they had added strength from being connected to the roots of other lily pads. This is the strength we experience if we are connected to those of the body of Christ.

Not only is this important to you as an adult, but also a sense of belonging to the body of Christ is crucial for your children. As children hear the songs of faith, see and hear adults praying for their needs and the needs of others, hear the scriptures read and participate in worship, their spiritual lives are being grounded, shaped, and rooted. All of us are formed and reformed spiritually by the act of worship.

Although my friend's granddaughter is just sixteen months old, she is already learning what it means to be a part of the body of Christ. Her favorite time in the worship service is when members of the congregation greet one another.

When Mattie hears the minister say, "Let us greet one another," she is the first one out of her pew. She races from person to person saying, "Hi, hi, hi." Although that is the extent of Mattie's vocabulary at the present time, she is using it all in extending hospitality to members of the household of God! When children, and adults as well, participate in the rituals of the church, there is a deep sense of being connected with God and with others. This sense of being interrelated and connected is vital to our spiritual growth.

9. Seek Spiritual Guidance Yourself

If we are seriously on the inward journey ourselves, we might seek a spiritual guide for our own life. We would want to be particularly attentive to whether the person we choose is also seeking a deeper spiritual life. Also the qualifications mentioned earlier in the section "What Does the Term Spiritual Guide Mean" are extremely important.

We have these wise words from Marjorie Thompson on the qualifications of a spiritual guide: "A spiritual guide need only be one who has traveled some distance along the path of the Christian life. A guide should be knowledgeable about the markers that lead forward on this path, as well as familiar with the pitfalls, detours, trials, and temptations along its course." She adds, "Such a person will reflect something of the character of Christ as a result of following in his way. A Christian who gives no evidence of humility, wisdom, compassion, or the ability to speak the truth in love will not likely be sought out as a spiritual guide."[15] These words should help us as we are attentive to God's leading as we seek a spiritual guide.

The guide might be someone from your church who is older and wiser and who has been on the spiritual journey for a long time. Many older adults in our churches would make excellent spiritual guides to younger persons. A spiritual richness interlaces the fabric of their lives, so just being in their presence can be beneficial to those who are earnestly seeking God.

Years ago young mothers gained much valuable knowledge from going to quilting bees, pea shelling sessions, and canning parties with older women. Young fathers had the opportunity to help in a barn-raising event or hay-baling sessions with their elders. But times have changed, and we no longer have time to sit together with neighbors or to talk at length with them. We rarely have the time to get together in groups, especially in intergenerational events. As a result, we often miss the wisdom, stories, and inspiration that in times past were shared during those times together. The loss is ours, and we must seek mentoring in other ways.

One great service that the church could provide is to offer training for older women and men to be mentors in the faith for younger women and men. Just to share in the richness and wisdom of an older person of faith would give encouragement and hope to younger persons who are struggling with life's journey.

A staff person from your church or from another church might also serve as a spiritual guide. Often these persons agree to become a spiritual guide to a limited number of people. You might ask your minister for suggestions for someone who is qualified as a spiritual guide or seek advice from friends and colleagues.

Above all, pray for guidance in this matter. In your prayers express your needs and ask God to send someone who will meet those needs. Watch for clues and signs as you meet and talk with people on a daily basis. Is this person the one God is sending to meet your need? Listen for God's prompting and nudging and leading. As you prayerfully watch and wait, in God's time someone who meets your needs as a spiritual guide will cross your path. If you need help in clarifying your needs, in knowing how to seek a spiritual guide, in understanding how to begin with a spiritual guide, several books in the bibliography (page 163) will be helpful to you.

10. Do Good Deeds for Others

Some of the earliest spiritual leaders considered doing acts of mercy essential if one was to mature in the spiritual life. Bernard of Clairvaux (1090–1153) said, "I will be spent for souls...We came not to be ministered unto but to minister." He continues, "Learn the lesson that, if you are to do the work of a prophet, what you need is not a scepter but a hoe."[16] Francis of Assisi wrote in a letter, "Being the servant of all, I am bound to serve all and to administer the balm-bearing words of my Lord."[17]

John Wesley felt that in order to grow spiritually one had to serve others. He insisted on the necessity of good works to maintain faithful discipleship and to sustain a relationship with God.[18] He made it clear to his members that there were good works to be done whether the members felt like it or not! His guidelines for serving Christ in the world are based on Matthew 25:35-36: to feed the hungry, clothe the naked, visit the prisons and the hospitals, and seek out those in need.[19] These are excellent guidelines for us as we enter into service for others. Our service might be as simple as taking food to someone in need or providing transportation for an elderly person. It might be serving a meal at a homeless shelter or volunteering in an inner city day care center.

One family that I know serves a meal at a homeless center during every Christmas holiday. They say that it is interesting to hear the comments in their family about this experience. Often, months later, the children cannot remember what gifts they received for Christmas. They do, however, remember serving the meal and talk all year about persons they met, how it felt to be there, or things homeless persons said.

Because God has blessed us so abundantly, we want to be a blessing to others. Because Jesus has commanded us to care for the poor and marginalized, we obey and teach our children the joy of following Jesus' commandments. In so doing our family will find that they are the ones who receive the blessing.

These ten spiritual disciplines, then, are examples of ways to place ourselves in God's presence so that God will be able to do what is necessary in our life, making it fuller and deeper spiritually. They are a means of receiving God's grace.[20] With God's help, we will be empowered with the strength and wisdom needed to take the pilgrimage of faith with our family. And as we, parents, grandparents and those who love children, are growing ourselves, we will be better equipped to guide the children entrusted to our care. "To spiritually feed, inspire, and support our children, we must keep spiritually feeding, inhaling and centering ourselves in God."[21]

Chapter Three

―――

Letting God's Light Shine Through

D o you remember the story of the little boy who was asked to define a saint? He thought for a few minutes. Then, remembering the stained glass windows at his church that portrayed images of the apostles, he answered, "Oh, I know who saints are. They are the people who let the light shine through." We as parents, grandparents, and special friends who want to be spiritual guides to children are certainly not saints, but we are those who let God's light shine through. We do this by letting God's light shine through our lives, our words, our thoughts and our actions.

What Does the Spiritual Guide Do for the Child?

Drawing from our earlier definitions of a spiritual guide, we will look more closely at these roles. We stated that a spiritual guide is on his or her own spiritual journey. In addition, spiritual guides are also:

1. Holy listeners
2. Amateurs who reflect Christ's love
3. Friends of the soul
4. Those who point beyond themselves to the kingdom

5. Companions in the difficulties and joys of life
6. God's ushers
7. Gateopeners for the Spirit

We Are Holy Listeners

Sometimes in parenting, we grow so weary in listening to our children. The chatter seems to go on for hours. But as a spiritual guide, we listen in a deeper way, with a deeper ear, or love's third ear, so to speak. We listen with the heart and with a goal in mind, waiting for the right moment to interject something of God into the conversation. We also look between the phrases and listen with discernment, trying to hear what God is saying to us about our children. We listen patiently trying to hear what our children are saying to us—what is it that they really mean?

Our grandson Samuel is at the jabbering stage in his talking. Often a distinct word comes through, but more often than not, his "talk" is just noises said in an interesting conversational tone. I find myself listening intently to him, waiting for those few clear words to come and then responding to him so that he will know that I have understood. In his "preverbal knowingness" he communicates with me.[1]

While speaking to the boy Samuel, God said to him, "See, I am about to do something in Israel that will make both ears of anyone who hears of it tingle" (1 Sam. 3:11). I think that often, if we listen closely enough, our children will say things that make both of our ears tingle. We must have the patience to listen for it.

Time is one of the greatest gifts we can give our children. I also know from experience that it is one of the hardest to give. Instead of seeing children as interruptions to our "real" life, if we have children, they are the real life—the main event. A greater sense of belonging and spirituality will occur when we take time to be with our children and truly to listen to them. We cannot listen halfheartedly if we are really to hear what the child is saying. Often it takes looking at facial expressions, observing body language, engaging in active listening, and using our intuitions really to hear what the child is saying.

With four children, I often grew tired of listening and of trying to meet everyone's needs. One day I was particularly distracted and fatigued. My three-year-old was sitting in my lap talking incessantly. I suppose he had grown tired of my occasional "uh huhs." Finally he reached up, put his little hands on my face and turned it toward him. He held it there, looking deep into my eyes until he finished his story. I got the message!

Susanna Wesley, the mother of John and Charles, gave birth to nineteen children, ten of whom lived to adulthood. She knew the importance of being with each child individually and set aside each week a special time for each child, to listen to her or him and talk with each one about the things of the spirit. What a wonderful thing it would be if we could set aside even an hour a week to be with each child. If there are several children in the family, let them know your plan of spending time with each one individually. This could be done on a Saturday morning for one child, perhaps having breakfast at a favorite place. For another it might be a Sunday night picnic or a walk through the park while being intentionally present to the child in every aspect of our being—mind, heart, and spirit. If the other children in the family know that their special time is coming, they will be willing to wait while their siblings have their time alone with their parents.

For children much of their learning takes place in the context of relationships. How we relate to the child or how we show love for the child speaks much louder than the words we convey. Spirituality is absorbed as well as taught. Through our holy listening, we are being spiritual guides for our children. And as we interact in our conversations with the child, we reflect Christ's love.

After Hannah fulfilled her promise and brought Samuel to the temple to live with Eli, Eli became the spiritual guide for Samuel. When God called to Samuel in the night, Samuel did not understand or recognize it as the voice of God. Three times God called, and still Samuel did not recognize God's calling. Often we are like that. We do not recognize God's voice or feel God's nudges, and we need another to help us understand God's work in our lives. As parents and grandparents, we have the opportunity of helping our children learn to recognize God's calling throughout all of life.

One great biblical example of a holy listener is Elizabeth, the mother of John the Baptist. We learn from the Gospel of Luke that after the angel visited Mary, telling her that she would bear the son of God, she went with haste to the hill country to visit Zechariah and Elizabeth. We do not know what went on during their visit together, but I can just imagine Mary sitting at the feet of Elizabeth, looking into her face, pouring out all the doubts and fears that were in her heart. I can see Elizabeth gazing intently into Mary's innocent face and saying to her words of courage and comfort: "If God has called you for this awesome responsibility, you can do it, Mary! If the angel said that with God nothing will be impossible, then that is the way it will be! Take courage, now, Mary, and don't be afraid."

Luke tells us that Mary stayed with Elizabeth three months and then returned home. I imagine that they had many conversations during her stay about the events that had taken place and would take place. Elizabeth must have been a holy listener for Mary, helping her to discern what the visit from the angel really meant for Mary and Joseph and for the whole world.

We have many opportunities in our children's lives in which we can be holy listeners for them. We can help them sort through events and feelings so that they can discern what God is saying to them. One way that we can do this is to help them acknowledge God's presence in all of life. For instance, if we are having a wonderful time as a family, we might simply say, "Isn't God good to prepare this happy time for us?" Or if we see a beautiful rainbow we might say, "Isn't God good to give us this beautiful rainbow?" Child developmentalists tell us that often children sense God's presence most acutely in the hard times (just as we adults do). But because God is with us at all times, in the good times and the bad, we want to provide hospitality for the presence of God in the good times too.

Gote Klingberg, a psychologist from Sweden, has identified four situations when children say that they think about God. From this study of 630 children the author lists these in order of frequency: (1) situations of distress, (2) experiences in nature, (3) moral experiences, and (4) formal worship experiences.[2] This is helpful information because it helps us to be on the alert during these types of experiences. We are then better able to help our children verbalize their experiences and find meaning in them.

It is also important in our conversations with our children that we share our own faith stories. We must be willing to say, "This is what I believe." Of course this needs to be done in a way that does not cut off conversation but in a manner that leaves room for discussion. It is good also to ask the child, "What do you think or feel about this?" The dialogue that takes place can be enlightening to both persons.

Often we learn a great deal about things of the spirit from our children. Once when I had an obligation to visit various businesses to request donations for my son's football team, I was fuming about having to do such a disagreeable chore (at least it seemed disagreeable to me). When my eleven-year-old daughter heard me, she said, "Mama, I think that Jesus said he would be with us always, and I think that means he will be with you this afternoon too." Her statement changed my whole day. I suddenly had a whole new perspective concerning what I was about to do. I actually enjoyed the afternoon, meeting new people and talking with them about the importance of being involved in the lives of our teenagers.

Children may be the model for adult spiritual development, rather than the other way around, as we often imagine. Perhaps "a task for adult spiritual development may be to recapture the child's more inclusive and all-pervading sense of relation to the spiritual which means that for them it is normally 'everyday' rather than dramatic."[3] Someone has said that God gives wise hearts to small children, and often it is from them that we learn about things of the spirit. After all, Jesus said that unless we become as little children, we shall not see the kingdom of God. Children can often be spiritual guides for us.

Children often ask questions for which we do not have answers, and we wonder how to respond to them. When this happens, it is all right to say, "You know, I don't know the answer to that, but we will try to find out together." John Westerhoff says that "what our children are really asking is for us to reveal and share ourselves and our faith, not to provide dogmatic answers. We do not need to answer our children's questions, but we do need to make our faith available to them as a source for their learning and growth."[4]

We Are Those Who Reflect God's Love as Seen in Jesus Christ

One biblical character who models for us a life that reflects God's love is Mary, the sister of Martha and Lazarus. There are three stories in the Gospels that help us know a little more about her. One comes from Luke 10:38-42 and tells of Jesus in the home of Mary and Martha. In this short scenario, Mary chooses to sit at Jesus' feet instead of helping Martha prepare dinner. This act was a radical violation of the social order of the day. To sit at the rabbi's feet was not the place for women; only men were granted that privilege. Yet Jesus does not chide her for doing this but comments that she has chosen "the better part." Mary's actions are a perfect example of what it means to "love the Lord your God with all your heart, and with all your soul, and with all your strength and with all your mind" (Luke 10:27).

Two stories from John also give us great insight into the personhood of Mary. The first tells of Jesus raising Lazarus from the dead (John 11:1–44). The second story recounts the story of Mary anointing Jesus at Bethany (John 11:55–12:11). In telling the story of Lazarus's death, John's account has the grieving Mary quietly and faithfully waiting for Jesus to come. She does not run frantically to meet him to tell of her grief. Instead she waits quietly, for she knows he will come. When he calls for her, she goes to him and falls at his feet, signifying great love and loyalty for him, knowing that he will meet her need. Later in John, Jesus is again in Bethany and at the home of Mary, Martha, and Lazarus. This time the dinner is in Jesus' honor. Martha is again serving, and Lazarus is reclining at the table with Jesus and the other guests. Mary takes about a pint of expensive perfume and pours it on Jesus' feet, wiping them with her hair. When Judas Iscariot objects to the waste, Jesus tells him to leave her alone. Mary, realizing that Jesus' earthly days are limited, responds to him in great love. Mary's life and action model the life of love that Jesus taught.[5] She also operates out of Jean-Pierre de Caussade's "sacrament of the present moment," and what a precious moment it is!

Margaret Guenther says that spiritual guides are those who reflect Christ's love.[6] Is this not what we as Christian parents endeavor to do daily with our children? Through our love we want the magnitude of God's love in Christ to shine through us.

We know that our unconditional love for our children is very important, because child developmentalists tell us that children's first image of God corresponds with their view of their parents. It is difficult for children to believe in God's unconditional love if they have not experienced unconditional love from parents, grandparents, or some other significant adult. Although we know that children's images of God change as they mature, their childhood image sets the stage for how they will view God throughout life.

Children often develop distorted images of God and Jesus, and as the spiritual guide for children in our care, our role is to listen for these distortions and offer correct interpretations. It is impossible to prevent all misinterpretations from occurring, but we want to eliminate as many of them from the child's mind as possible. An example of this might be the child who expresses a fear of God and feels that God is watching everything he or she does in order to punish any wrongdoing. When we hear this, it is our responsibility to speak to the child of God's love and God's care for us. We might talk about how God created us and all things and cares for each of us, even the small birds of the air. Or we could speak of how God created all the beautiful things of the earth for us to enjoy: the flowers and butterflies, rainbows and mountains, oceans and shells. And most of all, we could talk to the child about how God is a loving God who forgives us when we do wrong. Children need to know that we are human beings and we all make mistakes. But just as loving earthly parents forgive us, God forgives us too.

Another way we reflect the love of God as seen in Christ is in the way we treat others. Our children observe our interactions with those in our own household and with those around us. When we do good deeds for others, such as caring for the sick, taking food to the elderly, or telephoning a lonely person, children observe what we are doing. We can say, "Jesus told us to feed the hungry, so that's what I am doing." Or, "Jesus said to love our neighbors, so I'm doing that by taking them some brownies." If we live by the commandments of Jesus, children begin to understand the importance of doing good deeds.

Involving children in acts of kindness is a wonderful way for them to have some hands-on experience in following the way of Christ. They receive great joy in doing for others, no matter how small the task. To help prepare food to take to a needy family or to take flowers to a shut-in brings children a sense of accomplishment.

Two studies point out that doing acts of charity and kindness for others is a faith-forming event for children and teens. The Search Institute study (*Effective Christian Education* by Peter L. Benson and Carolyn H. Ekin) found that participating in acts of mercy and compassion is an important influence on the deepening of faith. As children and teens are involved in projects of caring, their own faith is strengthened.

A study by Merton P. Strommen and A. Irene Strommen shows that if the family is engaged in acts of caring and service, the children grow stronger in their faith. As children see the results of their efforts, they come to realize that God can use them at whatever age they are. It is important for them to know this. They do not have to wait until they are teenagers or adults to be used by God. To be involved in helping others gives children a sense of worth and strong moral purpose. It is interesting to note, too, that studies show participation in such acts of caring is a deterrent to undesirable and destructive behavior.[7] I believe acts of mercy, compassion, and kindness also help combat the selfishness which comes with the materialism and consumerism so prevalent in our society today.

David Hay says that "spirituality by definition is always concerned with self-transcendence. It requires us to go beyond egocentricity to take account of our relatedness to other people, the environment and...God."[8] As spiritual guides, we need to take a strong role in providing experiences for our children that help them look beyond themselves, their wants and desires, to the needs of others. There are many opportunities in our daily lives for doing this. You might take the child with you to visit an older adult in the nursing home, or permit the child to decide which of her or his outgrown clothes and toys to take to a homeless shelter. Help them understand, however, that we want to give items to others that are still in good condition, attractive, and usable. I will never forget helping to open boxes of used clothing that had been sent to a mission school where I was assigned. We were very excited to receive the boxes because many of the children in our area needed warm clothing. To our dismay, we found many of the coats had all their buttons cut off, and some of them were threadbare. Many of the toys in the boxes had broken pieces, absent wheels, parts missing or were rusted beyond repair. We want to encourage our children to share with others out of their plenty, not out of their leftovers.

You might also want to broaden the children's understanding of God's world by buying a current map or a world globe. When events in faraway places are mentioned in the news, help the child find that place on the map or globe. Then, during your prayer time with the child, pray for that location and the people who reside there. This stretches the child and helps him or her move beyond egocentric prayer to more altruistic prayer for others.

Spiritual Guides Are Friends of the Soul

One of the best biblical examples of someone who is a "friend of the soul" is Paul's relationship with Timothy. Paul loves Timothy as he would have loved his own son and refers to him as "my beloved child." He is concerned about the soul of Timothy and encourages him to remain faithful to the childhood training he received from his mother Eunice and his grandmother Lois. Timothy's spiritual well-being is always uppermost in Paul's mind (2 Timothy 1 and 2). Our own children's spiritual well-being should be of great concern to us also as parents, grandparents, and as spiritual guides for them.

We believe the soul to be that spiritual nature of a person considered in relation to God and regarded as immortal. As parents our major role is to see that the spiritual nature or the soul of the child is nurtured, just as we nurture their growth physically, intellectually, and emotionally. If the spiritual nature of the child is not growing, the child is not becoming all that God has created him or her to be. Barbara Kymes Myers has said that a self-confident spirituality is unlikely to develop in a child unless adults provide hospitable space for this to happen.[9]

How do we nurture this spiritual nature? We do this in the myriad of conversations we have with our child. We do it in the countless ways that we react with our child. We begin by cherishing the child and meeting the child's needs. We nurture the child as we take walks, as we play together, and even as we work out daily disputes.

We do not set aside times during the day and say, "All right, this is the time we will do spiritual nurture." Spiritual growth is a journey and takes a great deal of time and effort. We cannot be formed spiritually overnight, just as the child is not formed spiritually overnight. There is not for us or for our children a quickaholic spirituality!

The psalmist said "Wait for the LORD; be strong, and let your heart take courage; wait for the LORD!" (Ps. 27:14). We must be patient and wait for what we hope to see happen in our children's lives.

We must be careful not to set unrealistic goals either for our children or ourselves. Indeed, children are spiritual beings and seem to have an uncanny knowledge of God, a knowledge that we have not taught them. But we must not expect them to be "little saints" either. Children need to be children. They cannot always be expected to do the right thing, to behave perfectly, or at all times seek to do what God expects.

Our spiritual nature is always in process, and children must be left to be children until they have the maturity to advance in their spiritual life. David Hay makes an excellent point when he says, "The task of nourishing spirituality is one of releasing, not constricting children's understanding and imagination."[10] Children have an innate spirituality, and we want to provide experiences for it to flourish and grow.

We have to be careful that the experiences we choose for our children do not intimidate or overwhelm them. Gertrud Mueller Nelson illustrates this point well. She tells the story of a mother taking her young children to the seashore. They stand there facing the sea as the waves come crashing in one after another. Then, very deliberately, one child turns her back on this awesome and obviously overwhelming phenomenon. As she begins to dig a hole in the sand, she is soon joined by the other children. In a few minutes they let a little portion of the sea into their hole and begin to laugh and splash in it. In experiencing a small part of the huge ocean, they have come to terms with the sea in a way that made sense for them. That is, they have reduced it to a size they can comprehend. This is always true of children's awesome and mysterious experiences of the spiritual. They must come to terms with them in their own way and in their own time.[11]

A good way to provide spiritual nurture is to listen attentively to children's questions and to answer them as honestly as we can. Many of their questions reveal that they are trying to make sense of the universe and all they see. Where is God? Who made God? What does God look like? Where was I before I was born?

These questions are all good openings for discussing the life of the spirit, our connection to God, how God cares for us, and so forth. You might not know all the answers, but as has already been said, it is all right to say so. Share your own thoughts based on your experience, and use this opportunity for some discussion as to what the child believes. In getting insights from the child, you will take your cue as to where the discussion should go.

Another way to nurture the spiritual life of children is to pay attention to what interests them. What do they like? What captures their interest? If it is dinosaurs, become interested in dinosaurs yourself. Help children find books and other information about things that interest them. Show them how to research the subject that they are curious about, perhaps at the library or at home on the computer. All children should feel that they are competent in something, and your help is needed to make this come about.

Build your vacations around the things that your children are interested in. One year we went to the Alamo in San Antonio because our youngest son was interested in Davy Crockett. Since our older son was interested in sports, one year we visited a city where we could attend a major league baseball game. Another year we went to the mountains to camp and hike because our older daughter loved the mountains. The next year we went to the beach because our younger daughter loved the beach and enjoyed looking for shells. During vacation times like these, we can find many opportunities to speak to our children about God and of all that God has created in the world.

Some years ago I read an article that confirmed that the family table—eating together as a family—in homes across America was a thing of the past. The article stated that eating on the run was now the norm in our society since families were always on the go. The family dining table, no longer used for eating, now holds stacks of unopened mail or schoolbooks or lunch boxes.

If this is true in your home, I urge you to make a change. Psychologists now say that there are great benefits for children in sitting down and eating together as a family. Not only do children do better in school because of language development learned around the family table, but this practice also develops a sense of belonging and closeness with their family. It gives children a time and place to discuss things that have happened during their day and helps them learn to interact with one another in a positive way. Of course it goes without saying that the television must be off!

One of the side benefits of having the family eat together is that it can be a time for the family to work together in preparing, serving, and cleaning up after the meal. Children gain a great deal from feeling that they are contributing to the family unit in some way, and even the smallest child can do his or her part. The meal can be simple, but it is always fun to make it a ritual in some way. This could be done by having lighted candles, or decorating the table with some theme, or celebrating some event in the family. This is also a good time to start some traditions, such as holding hands as you pray, or taking a few minutes for each person to share something about his or her day, or have each member tell some current event, taking time to discuss it.

I know that schedules are difficult, but I would encourage you to eat together as a family several nights a week. These times will provide memories that the children will carry with them throughout life. Perhaps they will see the family meal as a tradition to carry on when they have families of their own.

Devotional times with our children also nurture their souls. Schedules are so busy for most families that it is difficult to find time for family devotions, but parents must be intentional in including this time together as a family. Perhaps you can only be together for devotional moments three nights a week, but even having devotions those three nights would be beneficial.

It may be that Saturday morning after breakfast, and before everyone scatters for various tasks, is a good time to have an extended family devotion. Make this a special time by having one child light a candle to represent God's presence. One child could read the scripture, another one could lead the prayer, and then Mom or Dad could lead a discussion about the meaning of the scripture. During the closing prayer hold hands, and at the close of the devotional time give a prayer of blessing to one another. Do this by hugging one another or by placing hands either on one another's heads or shoulders and offering a prayer of blessing, such as, "God bless you today" (or this week), or "May God's love and light shine upon you today," or "May the Lord bless you and keep you." Parents can bless children, children can bless parents, and children can bless children. There is no restriction on who can bless whom!

To invoke God's favor upon our loved ones or to confer well-being upon those we love is a meaningful act of love. To know that we are blessed by God and by those we love brings a sense of security and peace to our lives. It reminds us that we are spiritual beings who live in the promise and presence of God.

As we guide our children in the spiritual life, what we are doing is trying to help them become who God wants them to be and has created them to be. We try to provide as many opportunities as possible for them to explore all the opportunities that would lead them closer to God.

I remember when I was a child that on many summer evenings after dinner my brother and sisters and I would beg our mother to let us go outside to play for awhile before bedtime. After a hot, humid day we enjoyed playing hide-and-seek with our friends in the cool twilight hours. Usually my mother gave in to our pleas and permitted us to go, but as we left, she always said the same thing to us as we went out the door. "Don't go so far that you won't hear me when I call."

This is what we are trying to do as we nurture our children spiritually. We are trying to train them not to stray so far from God that they will not hear God when he calls.

Spiritual Guides Point beyond Themselves to the Kingdom of God

A good biblical image of one who pointed beyond himself to the kingdom of God is John the Baptist. You remember that when the Jews sent priests and Levites from Jerusalem to ask John who he was, he replied, "I am not the Messiah." The Gospel writer says that John came as a witness to the light of Christ so that all the world might believe in him. (John 1:8-9). According to John's Gospel, John the Baptist was careful to point out that his place in the scheme of things was subordinate to the place of Jesus, the Christ. John's function was always to point beyond himself to Jesus and the kingdom.

Parents have many opportunities in the normal flow of life to point beyond themselves to Jesus. We can lead our children into conversations about God and Jesus and about the realm of God of which Jesus speaks. Our function is subordinate to that of God's function in our children's lives. While we will be with them for a short span of their lives, we want them to have an ongoing, lifetime relationship with the One who has created them and brought them into being.

One of the ways that children come to know God as a loving presence in their lives is to hear the great stories of faith from the Bible. They need to understand that we have a great heritage with God, and the history of this heritage is found in the Bible. The people in the Bible were ordinary persons on a journey toward God just as we are. We find ourselves in their stories—sometimes in the triumphs, sometimes in the tragedies, sometimes in the failures, sometimes in the successes.

Of course we want to use stories from the Bible that are age appropriate and that have some meaning in the child's life. For the very young child, we want to tell them stories that speak of God's love and use stories from Jesus' life that express concepts of goodness and love. These are concepts that children can understand.

There are many stories, especially from the Old Testament, which would, of course, not be appropriate for young children. The story of Abraham being told by God to sacrifice Isaac is frightening to young children. The story of David's son Absalom being hanged by his hair in a tree would serve no purpose with children. We can, however, tell them stories from the Old and New Testaments that speak of goodness and mercy and God's great abiding love.

A place to begin is by showing the children your personal Bible and by turning to some of your favorite passages. You might say, "Because I love God and want to learn more about the teachings of Jesus, I want to read what the Bible tells us about them." You might, while holding your Bible, turn to a favorite story and tell it to the children in your own words. This might be the story of Jesus blessing the children or Jesus feeding the five thousand, or the friendship of David and Jonathan. Even if the children cannot read, they will understand that this is a very special book and that you treasure what is found within.

Bible storybooks are a wonderful tool in helping children know the stories of our faith. Many children choose a Bible story as their favorite story and will want it read time and time again. A word of caution about buying books for your children: Before you buy any book to give your child, read it first in its entirety yourself. Ask yourself these questions: Does this book give the image of God or Jesus that I want my child to have? Does it confirm my belief about who God is and what God does in our life? Are the pictures accurate for the story, and do they relate the nature of God that I want my child to have?

Recently I broke one of my own rules. I bought a Bible storybook about Noah's ark for a little friend. The pictures in the beginning of the book were lovely, showing the animals entering the ark two by two. However, after I got home, I was appalled to find near the center of the book a large, graphic picture of people struggling and gasping in the water during the flood. The looks on their faces were terrifying. This was definitely not a book I wanted to give to a young child!

We wonder why children want the same book read over and over again. We tire of the same one, but they never seem to. Children learn in many ways, and one of those ways is called *spiral learning*. Each time they hear a story they will hear it from a different viewpoint. And each time they hear it they will glean some new insight, some new meaning. So do not despair when children ask for the same story again and again. Just know that as they grow and develop, children are gaining new understanding each time they hear it read or told.

Because the Bible is the story of our faith, it intersects our lives in many ways. When we read of a Bible character who is faced with some problem, we relate to that story because we have problems too. When we hear of a Bible character receiving God's forgiveness and mercy, we take heart because we need forgiveness also. Children in their own way see these connections and draw these same conclusions. The Bible is the story of the journey of a people. Their story intersects with our own story and points us beyond ourselves to God who walks with us on our journey.

For several years there has been discussion about whether it is wise to have children memorize scripture verses. I believe that learning verses of scripture by heart is a good thing. Verses that are learned and tucked away can be pulled out at a later time when children might need them.

Not long ago I heard a man tell his story of being held prisoner for five years during a recent war. He said that during that time, the prisoners were not permitted to have books or Bibles, nor were they permitted to have paper or pens. They were only permitted to see fellow prisoners for a short period of time each day, so the days were long and lonely.

He and his fellow prisoners came up with a plan. Each of them during his time alone in his cell would try to remember as many verses from the Bible as possible. Then when they saw each other, they would share the verses they each remembered. The man said that it was amazing how many verses of scripture flooded their memories. Whole psalms often came back to them—psalms that they were not even aware of knowing.

After a period of time, the prisoners were permitted to have paper and pencils. Then from recollection they began to write down the verses and share them with one another. The former prisoner's testimony on the power of scripture to resurface and to give strength in a time of need was moving indeed. Similar stories could be told of persons in hospitals or nursing homes who, without being aware that they even knew certain verses of scripture, could recall them when they needed them most.

Certainly how we teach memorization is the key element. If we make it a disagreeable exercise and punish if it is not done in the way we deem satisfactory, then we are defeating the purpose. But if we work with our children, saying the verses with them, helping them find the verses in the Bible, writing or letting them write the verses on a card, then it can become a pleasant exercise. We need to be aware, however, that some children just cannot memorize. It is an almost impossible task for some. In cases like these, we do not want to make the children feel they have failed, but we try to help them learn key words or phrases that will be helpful to them.

Because we are a part of a great heritage, it is good to have children (those who are able) memorize the Doxology, the Gloria Patri, and the Lord's Prayer. These are so vital to our faith and connect the child to generations of Christians who have been singing or reciting or praying these statements of faith for centuries. In a recent lecture Dr. Charles R. Foster, a professor in Christian education, said he believes that by the time they are five years old, most children should know the words to the Lord's Prayer.[12]

Finally, if we want to point beyond ourselves to the realm of God, we must share our faith stories with our children. We tell them what God has done and is doing in our lives. We recall with them how God has been faithful to us all our lives by meeting our needs and by being a companion with us on the journey. We tell them of the times of struggle in our lives, and how we have drawn strength from God. We talk about how we are children of the promise: how God has promised to be our God, and how we have promised to be God's people.

Moses called the children of Israel to remember what God had done for them: "Remember this day on which you came out of Egypt, out of the house of slavery, because the LORD brought you out from there by strength of hand" (Exod. 13:3). "Remember the days of old, consider the years long past; ask your father, and he will inform you; your elders, and they will tell you" (Deut. 32:7). "Do not be afraid....Just remember what the LORD your God did to Pharaoh and to all Egypt" (Deut. 7:18). "Remember the long way that the LORD your God has led you these forty years in the wilderness" (Deut. 8:2).

Moses was constantly calling the people "to remember," and this is a word that we should use often with our children. "Remember what a good time we had at the church picnic?" "Remember how happy Aunt Ruth was to see us when she was in the hospital?" "Remember the Christmas play we did last year?" "Remember how sick grandpa was and now he is well?" The word *remember* helps us to recall and share our stories of faith and to praise God's faithfulness to us.

Moses also tells the Hebrew people to put these words in their heart and soul, and tell them to their children, talking about them when they are at home and when they are away, when they lie down and when they rise. The advice of Moses is good for us today because it speaks of ritual and repetition—day in and day out speaking of what God has done and is doing in our families. In doing this we point not to ourselves as parents or grandparents, but to God's glory and steadfast love.

Companions in the Difficulties and the Joys of Life

An example from the Bible of a classic spiritual friendship that endured the good and bad of life is that of David and Jonathan. The scripture says that "the soul of Jonathan was bound to the soul of David....Jonathan made a covenant (promise) with David, because he loved him as his own soul" (1 Sam. 18:1, 3).

Although Jonathan was the son of King Saul, his loyalty was to David, his dear friend. Saul tried to kill David on several occasions, yet Jonathan's love for David remained so steadfast that he warned David of the danger each time.

Later, after Jonathan's and Saul's deaths, David lamented for his faithful friend by singing a beautiful dirge.

Remembering his friendship with Jonathan, after his death, David took Jonathan's lame son, Mephibosheth, as his own (2 Sam. 9:1-13). This was contrary to the customs of that day, which required that all heirs of the former royalty be put to death. David's mercy was rooted in love for God and also in human love for his dear friend Jonathan. Their love survived the good and the bad of life.

Life was not without mountaintops or valleys for David, nor will it be for us as we go though life. It is unrealistic to think that just because we are seeking a deeper spiritual life for our children and ourselves that life will suddenly smooth out in front of us. This is just not the way it is. Life is life; there are the good times in families and the not so good times. There are the heartaches and the sorrows, the joys and the triumphs. Although our earnestness in seeking God's will for our families does not make life trouble-free, it does provide us strength for the journey. It gives us the assurance that we have a God in whom we live and move and have our being. And this makes all the difference!

I believe that one of the roles of the parent, grandparent, and others who love children is to offer hope to the child. To have meaning and purpose in life, even in the midst of difficult times, gives life the zest it needs for the living. To look to the future and say, "You are going to do great!" or "This is hard right now but it won't be this way forever" gives the child the assurance that you believe that life is good and has meaning and purpose. You project hope for a future that is in the hands of a loving God.

Our promise to God to be God's people is not just for the good times. Our promise to be the people of God "is binding when [we] enter into this relationship even (or perhaps especially) if later it becomes inconvenient or difficult to keep."[13] When we enter into covenant relationship with God, it is for all times, both in the good and the bad. One writer has said that when things got really bad for the children of Israel in their flight out of Egypt, they became " 'whiners in the desert' instead of being pilgrims en route to the promised land."[14] This is often our story as well.

Many years after their sojourn in the desert, Babylon took the children of Israel into captivity, and their beloved temple was destroyed. Their homes were demolished; their people forced into slavery. The people of God were left in a state of grief and despair. The prophet who wrote the Book of Lamentations spoke for all of them when he wrote:

> The thought of my affliction and my homelessness
> is wormwood and gall!
> My soul continually thinks of it
> and is bowed down within me.
> But this I call to mind,
> and therefore I have hope:
> The steadfast love of the LORD
> never ceases,
> his mercies never come to an end;
> they are new every morning;
> great is your faithfulness,
> "The LORD is my portion,"
> says my soul,
> "therefore I will hope in him."
> —Lamentations 3:19-24

Perhaps the majority of our children will not know the devastation that the Hebrew people experienced. There are, however, millions of our children who face incredibly difficult situations at an early age. Death, divorce, poverty, peer pressure, neglect, substance abuse, and feelings of meaninglessness are just a few of the issues that are a part of their lives.

The spiritual guide "calls to mind" or remembers for the family, just as the prophet did for the children of Israel, that the steadfast love of God never ceases; it is new every morning. As we awaken each day, we never know what special surprises God is going to bring into our lives, because God's mercies are new every morning.

We can say confidently to one child, "I know that you are hurting now, but things will be better." To another we might remark, "You have a right to feel disappointed right now, but next time things will work out better." And to a third, "God loves you and cares about your life."

Once when our family was going through a particularly hard time, we relied more heavily on God than usual. We turned to the scripture often, reading and re-reading verses with the children—verses that nourished and sustained us. We prayed about our situation, not knowing what the outcome would be. We tried to live the life of faith that said to our children, "We don't know how this will turn out, but regardless of the outcome, God is with us and that is what matters."

A noted psychotherapist and author, Polly Berrien Berends, has said, "A child who sees his parents take time for quiet, prayerful openness when they are in trouble or at a loss will learn that this is a resource for him as well."[15] I believe that this is true for our children today. They need to see us modeling the life of faith, even in—no, especially in—the difficult times of life. They need to see us being faithful to a steadfast God who loves us with an everlasting love.

Sometime after this event was resolved in our family, one of our sons said to me, "Mom, isn't it interesting that when we were the weakest as a family, we were the strongest spiritually?"

Paul says it this way:

My grace is sufficient for you, for my power is made perfect in weakness. So, I will boast all the more gladly of my weaknesses, so that the power of Christ may dwell in me. Therefore I am content with weaknesses, insults, hardships, persecutions, and calamities for the sake of Christ; for whenever I am weak, then I am strong (2 Cor. 12:9-10).

As spiritual guides, then, we want to give our children something that they can fall back on, something to steady them when the ground beneath them begins to shake.

A beautiful example of this might be the story that I heard recently of a boy whose family had to move abruptly from one town to another. The boy understood that his father's job required this, but that did not lessen the fact that he was having to leave all of his friends and a secure and comfortable place that he loved. His mother said that as she and her son followed the moving van out of town in their car, the boy sang a great deal of the way to their new location. The children's choir at his church, of which he had been a member, had been preparing for a special presentation, and he knew all of the songs by heart. During this difficult trek, he reached down within himself and pulled out words and melodies that would give his heart comfort.[16]

We are companions with our children—and with God— in the difficulties of life. We are there to smooth their hair and wipe away their tears and say those ancient words that are used by mothers everywhere, "There, there, it's all right. Everything's going to be all right."

I remember hearing my youngest daughter, Suzanne, utter those first soothing words to her newborn child as she came shrieking with terror into an unfamiliar world. "There, there, Chloe," she said as she cuddled her close. "It's all right. Everything is going to be all right."

"It's all right." Hebrew mothers probably spoke these words to their children as Herod's soldiers searched their houses in Bethlehem for baby boys. These were most likely words spoken by Jewish mothers as they gathered their children to their breasts in the boxcars that took them to the death camps during the Holocaust. These may well be the words that mothers use today as they hold their starving infants to dry breasts or words that fathers use as they usher their family out of the horror of a war torn village. They are still the words that mothers (and fathers and grandparents) say to their children when things go terribly wrong.[17]

In these instinctively murmured words of comfort, we do not deny the pain, uncertainty, or even the sometimes terror of life. We say them to remind the child—and ourselves—that at the deepest level of life, it is all right, for God is with us.[18]

My great-aunt Irene had no children of her own but she was always ready with a word of comfort for those in need. She had an expression that she used when things did not go as she or someone else had hoped or planned. As she smoothed and resmoothed her apron, she would say, "And that's all right too."

Julian of Norwich, a mystic who lived in England during the Middle Ages and spent much of her time in prayer, best expresses this concept. She had a beautiful way of proclaiming "an unquenchable optimism in God's power to bring good out of evil when she said, 'All will be well, and all will be well, and every kind of thing will be well.'"[19]

These beautiful words speak to us of God's abiding presence and love. By saying them we are not ignoring our children's pain, or the uncertainty or brokenness in our present situation, but we are saying that at the deepest level of our lives, in God's goodness and mercy, everything will be all right. As spiritual guides, this is the message that we convey to our children, not only by our words, but also by the very lives we live.

Not only are we spiritual guides with our children in the difficulties of life, but we are also companions with them in the joys of life as well. What a privilege it is to share their joy! Children exude happiness and are gracious enough to include us in it. To share in their giggles, their secrets, their funny stories, their rambunctiousness gives life new meaning for us. When my grandchildren come to visit, the world suddenly turns from black and white to Technicolor!

I have stated earlier that because child developmentalists have found that children sense God's presence more in the bad times than in the good (did they learn this from us?), we must work hard at bringing God's presence into the good times. This can be done in many ways. Helping the child be attentive to God might be as simple as saying, "Isn't God good to provide such a nice time for us?" or we might say, "I don't know about you, but when I look at this ocean, I feel God's presence very close to me."

It is also good to ask the child, "How did you feel when you saw the rainbow today?" or, "What were you thinking of when we were sitting out under the stars?" Often if we give children the opportunity with encouragement, they are willing to express their thoughts and feelings about God.

Another thing that we might want to do is to try to help the child be attentive to God in the everyday events of life. We might give each child several colorful stickers, such as butterflies or flowers, and ask them to put them in strategic places. This might be on their mirror in the bathroom, on their book bag for school, or on their lunch box. Then when they see the sticker, they are to remember that they are in God's presence.

We might also choose a word such as "bird" and tell them that anytime they hear this word, they are to think about God. I have also used a little bell with children and told them to listen for it as I ring it from time to time. When they hear it ring, they are to think of God. Children like to play games, and these activities are close enough to being games that they delight in doing them. Using a variety of ways to focus their attention on God during the happy times of life is beneficial. God is good and we want our children to associate God with all that is fun and beautiful and joyful.

Spiritual Guides Are God's Ushers and God's Gateopeners

When we try to think of someone in the Bible who was the epitome of God's faithful servant, someone who wanted to pass on the faith to one who came after him or her, who might that be? The person who comes to mind for me is Elijah, a colorful prophet of the Northern Kingdom in the ninth century B.C. His influence was so great that he shaped Hebrew thinking for centuries after his death. One day the Lord told him to seek out Elisha and to train him to be his successor (1 Kings 19:19-21).

Elijah was obedient and found Elisha in a field plowing with twelve oxen, and he went up to him and threw his mantle upon him. Evidently Elisha knew the meaning of this ritual because he understood that by this action he was being called by God. He told his parents and friends goodbye, left with Elijah, and they began a fruitful ministry together.

The transfer of spiritual leadership from the elderly Elijah to the youthful Elisha is a beautiful story. Some time after they had been together, Elijah knew that the time was near when he would be taken up to heaven. As they traveled on that last day Elijah tried repeatedly to get Elisha to stay behind while he went on further, but each time Elisha refused and continued the journey with Elijah.

Finally Elijah asked Elisha, "Tell me what may I do for you before I am taken from you?" And Elisha's beautiful answer was, "Please let me inherit a double share of your spirit." Elijah explained to him that this was a hard request. Yet Elijah said that if Elisha saw Elijah as he was being taken up to heaven, he would inherit Elijah's spirit. Soon after, a chariot and horses of fire took Elijah up in a whirlwind into heaven, and as Elisha saw it, he cried out after his beloved mentor and spiritual guide. It has been said that only to the preeminently spiritual was such a vision possible. Elijah had trained him well. Elisha picked up Elijah's mantle that had fallen, went back across the Jordan, and took up his ministry. Elijah was God's usher, a gateopener to the Holy Spirit for Elisha (2 Kings 2:1-15).

As an usher and gateopener for God, we try to provide time and space for God to enter the child's life. Of course

God is already there, ready and willing to communicate with our children, but they must learn to be open to God's leading. Someone has said that the winds of the Holy Spirit are blowing, but we must hoist our sail. We must teach our children to be attentive to God's still, small voice in their hearts.

One of the ways we as spiritual guides can help our children is to provide time for silence and solitude. Just as a person who lives in a polluted environment must find clean air for a healthy body, those of us who live in constant noise and confusion must find solitude and silence to have healthy souls. Polly Berrien Berends says that "the importance of quiet time is something that our culture fails to respect...thus we teach our children to fear silence and solitude—or at the very least we distract them from it."[20]

Although we have been led to believe that children do not like to be quiet, some studies show the contrary. When children are encouraged to have silence, not as punishment but as a time of reflection, they enter into it with awe and mystery. I encourage parents and other persons who love children to invite their children to find a quiet space that just fits them. In warm weather this can be under a bush, in a tree, behind a fence. In cold months this could be in their room, under their bed, behind a door, or in their closet. Encourage them to have their quiet time and space to listen to what God is saying to them.

Of course one of the most important ways that we open the gate for the Holy Spirit in our children's lives is by teaching them to pray. When we teach our children to pray, we are enabling them to have an ongoing relationship with God. We are helping them know that they can use their own words to talk to God and to listen to God at any time, in any place, and about anything.[21]

The earliest prayers that children pray are prayers of praise and thanksgiving. This comes naturally to them and should always be encouraged. As they grow and develop in their spiritual lives, they, of course, add other forms of prayer—prayers of confession, forgiveness, intercession, and petition.

We teach our children to pray best by modeling the life of prayer for them. When they see and hear us praying, they know that we believe in the power of prayer and that we find comfort in communicating with God. As they see us praying, children are quick to model our behavior.

It is important to have set times of prayer with our children, such as mealtime and bedtime, but we also must encourage them to pray whenever they have a need. They do not have to wait until bedtime prayers to pray for a need that they might have on the playground in the morning. To help children know that God's love and presence surround them constantly, in the good times and the bad, is one of the greatest gifts that we can give them.

We can act as God's usher by helping our children learn to journal their journey with God. Of course they must be old enough to write and to form sentences, but when they are able, this is an excellent way to help children connect their daily lives with their Creator. A journal is not a diary listing their everyday activities; it is a time to record their encounter with God, asking "Where have I seen God today? Where has God been active in my life?" As they write a sentence or two about their interaction with God, they begin to see that all of life is connected to God.[22]

With all of the societal issues that impact the family today, especially our hurried lifestyle and our sense of dislocation, it is often our traditions and rituals that are eliminated first from our lives. How sad this is because these are the things that help give life meaning for us and for our children. Mary Pipher in her book *The Shelter of Each Other: Rebuilding Our Families*, says that when families become too busy, the first thing eliminated is ritual. She concludes that families often need help building rituals into their lives.[23]

In the Christian faith we are blessed because we have many rituals already in place for us if we would use them·

saying grace and using rituals surrounding meals and celebrating rituals around the festivals of the church year, including Advent, Christmas, Epiphany, Lent, Easter, Pentecost, and
Kingdomtide. One helpful resource is *Living in God's Time: A
Parent's Guide to Nurturing Children Throughout the Christian
Year* by Margaret McMillan Persky. In her book she gives
suggestions about how families can use the liturgical seasons
of the church year to enrich their spiritual lives.

Other rituals and celebrations such as birthdays, baptisms,
weddings, and family reunions should, for the Christian, be a
time of remembering God's goodness to us. These and other
rituals need to be continued in our families so that children
will know, "This is what we do in our family." These structures
are very important to children and the whole family unit.

Finally, when I speak of the spiritual guide as being one
who is an usher or gateopener to God's Holy Spirit, I do not
mean that the whole burden of whether or not the child has
a spiritual life is your responsibility alone. You can provide
hospitality for the Holy Spirit, and you can make sacred
space for the child to encounter God, but you cannot make
the spiritual life happen. The relationship between God and
the child is God's work, and you only need to be faithful in
doing your part.

I remember a story that a young mother told me once. She
wanted so badly for her two young children to have an experience of God. One day it had rained in torrents all morning.
She and the children were tired of being in the house and
were bored with what they were doing. The mother went to
the window and discovered that the rain had stopped. She
looked out across the lawn, and in the distance she saw a
beautiful rainbow. Sensing that this could be a meaningful
experience for the children, she rushed to help them put on
their boots and coats so they could go for a walk. She hoped
that in the process, they would discover the rainbow and that
it would be a moment of worship and inspiration.

Much to her dismay, however, the children were cross and dawdled as they put on their rain gear. Their scattered toys distracted them, and they were frustrated as they made their way to the door. Finally as they started down the steps and into the yard, the mother was disappointed to see that the rainbow had vanished. Since they were outside anyway, she decided to make the best of the situation and allow the children to play in the puddles in the yard. Soon they were having a good time!

Later as they started to go back into the house, the little boy, who was four, and his sister, who was two, started up the steps together. As they did, their eyes caught a spider web that was sparkling with raindrops in the sun, displaying an array of beautiful colors. An exquisite butterfly had lighted nearby, spreading its wings in glorious splendor. The little boy stopped suddenly, noticing the beautiful sight. Then he said quietly to his little sister, "You know, don't you, that God made this butterfly and this spider and the rain and everything in the world?" There was a hushed silence and then his sister whispered in her small voice, "Yes, I know." The mother said that she could not have orchestrated a more spiritual moment if she had tried.[24]

You do not need to do it all. God is with you as you make time and space in the child's life for the Holy Spirit to work. You are just God's usher, God's gateopener.

Chapter Four

————

Grandparenting as a Gift

Grandchildren are the crown of the aged," so says the writer of the Book of Proverbs (17:6). And what a joy these children are to the even "not so aged" grandparents! After the strain and stress of raising our own children, it is such a delight to be with our grandchildren without having the day-to-day responsibility. Perhaps the stress of making ends meet financially, the issues of discipline, the countless daily tasks, and the health factors and concerns have all prevented us from enjoying our own children to the fullest. Now we have the golden opportunity of playing with and loving our grandchildren without these overwhelming responsibilities. This opportunity is not just possible for those who have grandchildren of their own but is a joy that can be shared by any seasoned adult who loves children.

Joe Horrigan, a child psychiatrist, says that grandparents are in a privileged position; they can give the "goodies" without giving the "baddies." And how much fun it is to do just that! He continues, "Ideally the role of grandparents is positive re-enforcement: giving praise, hugs and kisses, and emotional encouragement. And they can teach children that the generations are important, that there is a connection not only to their parents but to another generation as well.

Grandparents are a store house of the family history and traditions and they need to confer this on the kids."[1]

It is interesting to note the changing concept of grandparents that has come about over the last few years. If you think of your own grandparents, what do you remember most vividly? A grandmother who was always home sewing or cooking and a grandfather who worked in the yard or garden or whittled interesting things?

As I think of my grandparents, I recall my grandmother being in the kitchen cooking wonderful things for us to eat, especially her famous angel food cake with its inch-tall white icing. I recall my grandfather sitting in his chair reading or talking with us about various issues in life or teaching us to play checkers. I also remember them reading the Bible to us and having family prayer.

Many grandparents do not fit this mold today; and that is all right. Some grandparents have very busy, active lives that have caused us to rethink our stereotypical view of grandparents. For instance, some grandmothers do not cook anymore, but they know how to order a great pizza! Some grandfathers are busy playing golf or pursuing other interests but find time to include their grandchildren in those or other special events. Some grandparents are still working full-time and have to be creative in finding time to spend with their grandchildren.

The new generation of grandparents comes in many varieties: old and young, active or sedentary, involved in many activities of their own or content to be at home and available to their children and grandchildren. Regardless of the diversity, the role of the grandparent has changed little over the years. Grandparents continue to be those senior members of a family who are the stable role models for the younger generations.

Although grandparents are able to fulfill many roles, I believe there are five main roles that grandparents fulfill today: to be present in the lives of their grandchildren, to love them unconditionally, to connect the generations, to provide emotional, physical and spiritual support for their grandchildren's parents (their own children) and last, and perhaps most important, to be a strong spiritual guide for their grandchildren.

To Be Present in the Life of the Child

For those grandparents who live in close proximity to their grandchildren, being present in the life of the child is not a difficult thing to do. These grandparents may be available for baby-sitting, for attending school functions, for taking the children places they need to go, and so forth. It is natural in this setting to see their grandchildren on a regular basis, sometimes even daily.

There are those grandparents, however, who do not live near their grandchildren, and this presents other challenges. The grandparents and the family with children must be willing to make some sacrifices in order to see each other on a regular basis. Being with the grandparents is so important in the lives of children that it is worth the effort. The feeling of belonging to a wider family unit helps give security and solidarity in the child's life, and this in turn helps when the storms of life come.

One family I know is separated from one another by several hundred miles. Yet they have made a vow to see one another at least once every six weeks. This has not been easy to do, but they have been faithful to their vow, which has worked well for them.

There is another group of grandparents that I must address now. These are the ones who long to see their grandchildren and, for reasons beyond their control, cannot. They are ready and willing to make any sacrifice in order to be with them but are refused permission to do so. Unfortunately, because of some family break, whether that is divorce or death or some schism within the family unit, the grandparents are not permitted to see their grandchildren. This brings on much heartache for the grandparents and for the grandchildren.

In cases such as these, the main thing that the grandparents can do is to pray for the children and their parents. If you find yourself in this situation, try to think of ways to maintain a spiritual connection with your grandchildren. One way to do this is to place pictures of your grandchildren in your place of prayer, and each day, as you are having your devotions, pray specifically for your grandchildren. Even if pictures are not available, you can still pray effectively for them.

If you are in this group of grandparents and are permitted to write your grandchildren, try to keep an ongoing communication with them. Be careful not to write anything that would be offensive to the parents because doing so could suddenly cut off communication. In your letters tell your grandchildren what you are doing, and talk about things that the child is doing. Do you know their best friend's name, what the children are particularly interested in, how they spend their time after school? These would all be subjects that could keep the conversation going between you and the grandchildren.

Send small gifts to the child from time to time if you are permitted to do so. Make the gift as appropriate as possible. If you are sending clothing and have not seen the child in some time, ask a friend who has a grandchild about the same age as your grandchild what styles of clothing children are wearing. This would help you in your choice of gifts.

Another thing you might do is to keep a notebook or journal for the child. In it you could put things that you remember about your ancestors, information the child someday might like to know. You could write about the child: how you remember his or her birth, what your hope and dreams are for him or her, how you have prayed for him or her over the years, and how you have longed to see him or her.

Occasionally during your time of prayer and meditation, identify a verse from the Bible that speaks to you about this particular grandchild. Note this in the margin of your Bible and record it in your notebook. Perhaps someday, in God's time, this journal might become the possession of your grandchild and would let the child know how much you have loved her or him over the years.

Another group of grandparents that should be mentioned might be called the "runaway grandparents" or the "fun-seeking grandparents." These are those grandparents who have labored to meet a lifetime of responsibilities, and when retirement comes, they move away from their families, seeking fun and adventure. They might even say, "We've worked hard all our lives. We deserve to have some fun and this is what we are going to do."

Please do not misunderstand me. I am not talking about all grandparents who move to a better climate, or who take fun trips to various parts of the world. Persons who have worked hard all their lives deserve to have some carefree, happy days in retirement. But at the same time, grandparents need to remember their responsibility to the next generation. One writer has said that "children are living messages we send to a time we will not see. We must do everything we can to make sure that those messages are connected to God and to family and are full of hope."[2]

If we are to fulfill this mandate we must be present in the lives of our grandchildren on an ongoing basis. Connecting with them once a year will not be enough to make this happen. We must make an effort to be an ongoing part of their lives.

According to Dr. Horrigan, "the 'Me' generation is not limited to a certain age group. Older adults who are grandparents often fit into this group. Life for some of them has been tough, but life is not about finishing up the story with 'and we went to the beach and lived happily every after.'" In cases like this, he even advises parents to say to the grandparents, "Look, it would really be nice to have you more actively involved in our children's lives."[3] This, I think, is a legitimate request.

Again, let me say that I am not referring to all grandparents who move away from their children and grandchildren seeking a better climate or a more relaxed lifestyle, or to those grandparents who take extended travel time after retirement. I have known many families who do these things and still maintain a strong, viable relationship with their grandchildren. One family with which I am acquainted visits their grandchildren on a regular basis as well as has the grandchildren visit them. They faithfully keep up with birthdays, graduations, and other special days.

One set of grandparents that I am aware of has done an excellent job of keeping up with their grandchildren by e-mail as they have traveled around the country. This has been an exciting thing for their grandchildren to maintain contact with their grandparents and to learn about all of the exciting places they are visiting. The travels of the grandparents have enriched their grandchildren's lives.

Another group of grandparents, and the numbers in this group are growing yearly, are grandparents of blended families. A friend told me that two of her grandchildren have four sets of grandparents. She said that there is never a school event, a sports activity or a program at the church in which these children are involved that two or more grandparents are not there to support them. "This is great," she said. "I don't think any child can have too many grandparents." Of course there could be problems in situations like this, but when all adults work together, this could work in the best interest of the child.

One group of grandparents that we do not hear much about, and this is a small group, are grandparents who live with their children and grandchildren. This used to be the norm in our society, but it is getting to be a rare phenomenon, as there are very few three-generation households anymore. My husband's grandmother lived with his family until she died, and this was a wonderful experience for the grandchildren. His grandmother told them stories, taught them Bible verses, and was a contributing member of the household. Some of my husband's fondest memories are of his grandmother.

One last important group of grandparents are those who have the responsibility for rearing their grandchildren. The number of grandparents who fit this category is also growing each year. Daunting responsibilities accompany this role causing these grandparents to become full-time caregivers, not by choice but by necessity. A death, divorce, serious illness, or some other difficult circumstance often places grandparents in the role as full-time guardians. When this happens, the grandparents must assume, along with all the myriad other responsibilities of parenting, that of being the primary spiritual guide for the child or children in their care. At the close of this chapter we will look at some specific ways that all grandparents can be spiritual guides for their grandchildren.

To Love Grandchildren Unconditionally

Many of us, when we look back on the busy days of rearing our children, have some regrets. We do not say, "I wish I had kept my house cleaner," or "Oh my, I wish that I had ironed more play clothes." No, the thing that we regret the most is that we did not spend more time with our children, did not express our love for them more, and sometimes forgot to show them unconditional love.

When our children were small, we were so tired, so filled with angst about being the perfect parent or about doing the right thing, that we forgot to express our love adequately. It is not that we did not love our children. I know that I loved mine fiercely, but I also know that I often let the mundane things of life become the important issues. Clean rooms, clean clothes, meals on time became all important. As a friend of mine says, "I forgot to let the main thing be the main thing." This is true with many parents. The main thing, of course, is our children and our relationship with them. Children should not be seen as interruptions to the main thing of life; they are the main thing. John Westerhoff says that often we value children for who or what they can become, instead of who they are right now.[4] This very moment is a valid time in the life of the child and should be cherished as such.

As grandparents it is as if we have been given a second chance to love unconditionally. Not that we have been given a second chance to be a parent; no, that is the parent's responsibility, and we must not interfere with this sacred role. But we do have a second chance to love our grandchildren and to love them unconditionally. With God's help, perhaps we will do a better job this time around.

I read once that every child deserves to have someone who loves him or her outrageously. That is a role that most of us can fulfill and fulfill very well. Many new grandparents have said to me, "I didn't know that I would love my son's child this much. I am in love with this little angel and can't seem to stop myself from doing all the crazy things that grandparents do." I answer, "You know, I think this is just wonderful. Every baby deserves to have this kind of love."

To love our grandchildren does not mean that we agree with everything that they say and do. We do not give in to their every wish. Our grandchildren need to see us standing firm in our values and in what we believe. As grandchildren get older they may disagree with us, but they need to know what we stand for and what we hold sacred. Just as our grandchildren are hungry for our love and attention, they are hungry for guidelines by which to live. By the lives we lead, grandparents can model for their grandchildren lives that exemplify faith in God, strong values, respect for all human beings, and a sense of self-worth.

There has perhaps never been a more difficult time for children to grow up, and many children are filled with fears and insecurity about the future. Many lack self-esteem and many are faced with tough peer pressure and overwhelming temptations. We, as grandparents, can be a stable force in their lives, giving them the reassurance and support they need.

We can let them know that we are always there for them and that we believe in them. Even though they might do some things that we do not approve of, we can say, "You know, what you did troubles me, but that doesn't mean that I don't love you. Nothing you could ever do would make me stop loving you."

The unconditional love that grandparents shower on a child can give her or him just the strength needed to get through life. My grandparents did not show partiality toward their grandchildren, but I always knew, without a doubt, that I held a special place in their hearts. By a touch, a hug, a word, a letter of encouragement, they could change my feelings about myself and make me see life in a more positive way. They gave me a sense of security and hope regardless of life's circumstances. Their love was a sustaining force in my life.

We can do this for all our grandchildren, whether we have one or ten, whether we live near them or far away. Our hearts are big enough to have all the love we need to go around. There is a wonderful verse in 2 Timothy 1:5-7 that speaks of what we can do as grandparents for our grandchildren. Paul says to Timothy:

> I am reminded of your sincere faith, a faith that lived first in your grandmother Lois and your mother Eunice and now, I am sure, lives in you. For this reason I remind you to rekindle the gift of God that is within you through the laying on of my hands; for God did not give us a spirit of cowardice, but rather a spirit of power and of love and of self-discipline.

We do not have to be timid about showing unconditional love for our grandchildren because this love will remain with them even after we are gone.

To Connect the Generations

As grandparents we stand in an unusual position. We have knowledge of at least five generations. We have information about our own grandparents and parents, knowledge about our children and ourselves and now knowledge about our grandchildren.

This is an awesome stance! Often though, because of our hurried lifestyles, the distance that separates families, the lack of communication and the disinterest in family-related issues, many of the wonderful stories of our families do not get passed on from generation to generation. Who has not felt some regret after an older member of our family has died, regret that we did not ask them some of the information about our family that we wanted badly to know but waited too long to ask?

One of the greatest things that we can do for our grandchildren is to share our family stories with them. As children hear these stories, they will come to recognize who they are in the family structure. They will develop a sense of self in the midst of the greater family and come to see themselves as part of a larger family.

Recently my little granddaughter, Chloe, visited me. We were in an upstairs bedroom and I laid her on the bed. Then I remarked to her mother, "You know, don't you, that Chloe is in the house that her great-grandfather built (my husband's father), and is lying on a bed that belonged to her great-grandmother (my mother), on a quilt that was made by her great-great-grandmother (my mother's mother)!" It was quite a moving moment.

One way to preserve family history and stories is to invest in a small tape recorder and tape these stories at your convenience. They could then be shared with our grandchildren at an appropriate time. It would be helpful to make several short tapes rather than one lengthy one because of children's attention span. You could share with your grandchildren stories about your grandparents, your home of origin, where your ancestors came from, where your mother got your name, and many other exciting stories from your past. Your grandchildren will find them exciting whether you do or not!

In most families there are favorite stories that are repeated over and over at each family gathering. Someone will invariably say, "Tell us again about Uncle John's encounter with the bull," and that starts the stories flowing. The ritual of storytelling is one that needs to be revived and cherished in our families.

In our family I always asked my mother to tell about when she was young and often drove my grandfather's car for him. He was a minister of a rural church, and in the afternoons went from house to house visiting the members of his congregation. He did not particularly like to drive a car, so she often acted as his chauffeur. One afternoon she went into a house to visit with him, and when they returned to the car, a cow had stuck her nose in and chewed up part of my grandfather's Bible. We still have that Bible in our family today, and I tell my children and grandchildren this story.

My young grandson gave me a lovely book one Christmas (bought by my son and daughter-in-law, I am sure). In it are beautiful pages for me to fill in and give back to Samuel some day. There are pages for the family tree, space for information about my mother and father, pages for information about my early years, a place to record how I met my husband, a place for favorite family recipes and ample space for pictures. It will be a way that Samuel can learn about his wider family and a book he will treasure in years to come.

You do not have to buy a special book for this type of information. You can just choose a good, inexpensive notebook and decorate it yourself, using your own artistic talents. The important thing is to start recording in it soon and add to it from time to time. Present it to your grandchild on some special birthday or occasion.

The most important thing to remember in the process of connecting the generations, however, is to relate your story to "The Story," God's story, sharing with your children and grandchildren how God has been with you on your life's journey. Just as God was with God's people in the Bible, God will be with us today. Just as God was with our great-grand-mothers and great-grandfathers, God will be with our chil-dren and grandchildren.

Our grandchildren need to know that we truly believe this. Our God is a God of faithfulness and steadfastness and will accompany us all along life's journey. We need to tell specific stories of how God has been present in our lives, in the good times and the bad.

Another way to connect the generations is by singing songs that have been sung in your family for generations. One night rather late our phone rang. It was my son Tim saying, "Mom, you remember that song that you used to sing to us? I think it was 'Froggy went a courting and he did ride, uh hum' or something like that.'" I did remember the song and gave him the words. My grandmother sang it to both my mother and to me, and I sang it to my children. Now my son is singing it to his son.

In addition to fun songs, my grandmother and mother sang many songs of faith for me and for my siblings. The words to those songs became imbedded in my subconscious, and often, still, they come back to me today. Two of them are "Tell Me the Stories of Jesus" and "Count Your Blessings, Name Them One By One." I sang those same songs to my children, and I hope they are singing them, or other songs of faith that they choose, to their children.

My grandmother was very intentional about some of the things that she did for us. She wanted her grandchildren to know the name of the river that ran through the city where she lived. She wanted us to visit museums and know some-thing about art and the cultural world. She felt it was impor-tant for us to know the names of flowers and trees. She wanted us to be able to meet and speak properly with peo-ple. And she saw that we had occasions to learn those things.

Often as we were on the way to one of these places or events, she would say to us, "Remember now, we are building memories. Remember, we are building memories to last a lifetime." As grandparents this is one of the special things that we can do for our grandchildren—we can build memories with them to last a lifetime.

To Provide Emotional, Physical, and Spiritual Support for the Parents of Our Grandchildren

The harried life of our children greatly influences the lives of our grandchildren. In our society today, we think we must fill every minute with something. There is no time to sit on the porch and rock and watch the birds. There is no time to lie in the grass and stargaze or moon watch. If we are not doing *something* we think that we are being unproductive.

Our children keep up this pace year after year, and our grandchildren are caught up in the frenzy. Our adult children need help that only we can give them. They need us to say to them, not "hurry up," as we did when they were children, but "slow down." "Enjoy life, relish your children, take time for the important things of life." Unfortunately, if we have not modeled this kind of life for them, our advice often falls on deaf ears. Even so, our children need to hear us say these words, and we hope they will begin to take them seriously.

Of course, we have to be careful how we give advice or it can be misunderstood. Certainly we do not want to be over-bearing or authoritative with our advice. But if, in a quiet way, we remind our children that life is precious and passes too quickly, we might be able to help them bring some balance into their hectic lives.

Another thing that we can do for our children is to share with them some of the physical challenge of caring for their children. Occasionally we can stay with our grandchildren and give our children a night out. From time to time, even if they live at a distance, we can take care of our grandchildren while their parents have a more extended time apart.

How much our adult children need time for quiet and re-creation of the soul! After a few days apart from their children, they begin to see life with a different perspective. They are able to see new ways to make parenting more manageable and less stressful. Just as their children need time and space to become who God is calling them to be, so do our adult children. We, then, can be instrumental in allowing time and space for them to connect with their inner selves and with God.

We can also give our adult children words of encouragement and hope. If we recall when our own children were small, it meant a great deal for someone to say to us, "You are doing a great job with your children" or "I know you are tired, but eventually you will see that nurturing these children has been worth it," or "Hang in there—don't give up." These words were especially meaningful if they came from our own parents. Their approval meant more to us than the approval of anyone else.

By E-mail, by phone call, by fax, by letter or by dropping an occasional card to our children, we can encourage them along the pilgrimage of life. These messages can relay to them that you believe in them and that they have your love and support. Just knowing that you are thinking of them will mean so much.

I would like to say a word about writing letters to our children. Yes, real old-fashioned letters written by hand with pen and ink! I know that this takes time, but there is something very special about seeing the handwriting of someone we love on an envelope addressed to us. Another wonderful thing about letters is that we can keep and read and reread them over the years.

Years ago when I lived far from home, I remember how I used to feel when I would receive a letter from my mother. It meant, I knew, that she had taken time from a busy life to write me a few lines, and that always meant so much to me. My father seldom wrote, but I still have two of his letters (most likely the only two he ever wrote me). They came at a time in my life when I was feeling overwhelmed with all the challenges of raising my four children and a word from him meant so much.

The father of a friend of ours lived in a distant city. Our friend told us recently that his father, who was a busy doctor, took time each week to write a letter to him. Peter cherished those letters and looked forward to them weekly.[5] Sometimes we can say more on the printed page than we can in a telephone conversation, and our words seem more lasting because they can be kept and looked at again and again.

Another important thing that we can do for our adult children is to pray daily for them—and some days pray for them many times a day! Our role now that they are grown is not to tell them what to do or how to lead their lives or how to raise their children. We have no more authority over their actions. That time has passed. What we can do now is to commit their lives to God, asking God to be their wisdom, their strength, and their shield. The responsibility is God's now, and God can do what we can no longer do for our children. It is a comfort to know that God can do far more abundantly than all that we ask or think.

Last, one of the things we must remember about our adult children is that they need our love too. Often without thinking, we are so enamored with our grandchildren that we bypass our children in showing love. We rush to our grandchildren to greet them and give hugs and kisses, overlooking our children. But we are all human beings who never outgrow our need for our parents' love. It is normal for us as grandparents to have great love for our grandchildren, but we must remember that our own children need our love, respect and appreciation also. Shower that love on your children as well as your grandchildren.

To Be a Strong Spiritual Guide for Our Grandchildren

One of the strengths of grandparents, I believe, is that they have the uncanny ability to see each child as an individual and are able to value the gifts of each one. Howard Rice says that part of the task of any spiritual guide is to recognize human uniqueness and to respect and value each person's particular pilgrimage.[6] This is something that grandparents do well. We see each child for who she or he is and respect each child's particular pilgrimage in life.

Someone has said that parents today are so busy giving their children things they did not have as children that they fail to give them the important things they did have, such as uninterrupted time together, visiting neighbors and friends, doing good deeds for those in need, and providing strong values including kindness, compassion, honesty, and feelings of self worth.

These are the things that grandparents specialize in. Grandparents come to the role of grandparenthood with knowledge and wisdom from their years of living. They have already come through several stages in life and are beginning to understand what it is that makes life meaningful. After all, to find meaning in life is one of life's most difficult quests. It is hoped that after years of living, we have come to the place where we understand the source of this meaning of life. We as grandparents are privileged to share some of life's wisdom with our grandchildren.

We must remember that we are not concerned specifically with teaching grandchildren long lists of data to memorize and give back to us (though they might learn some in the process). We are not trying to teach them theological theories and concepts (though they might learn some in the process). Our connection as grandparents to grandchild is spiritually based. We communicate at another level and many times without words. Ours is the domain of the inner child.[7]

In the preface to *Holy Listening*, by Margaret Guenther, Alan Jones says that grandmothers and grandfathers can play an important part in soul-making. He applauds Guenther's use of the image of the Appalachian granny woman who is wise, resourceful, and experienced. Her role is to assist in the birth of babies who are born in the remote and hard to reach areas of the mountains. "We need spiritual grannies and grandpas who have the time and the wisdom to wait patiently in out-of-the-way places of the spirit and quietly bring new things to birth in others."[8] This is a challenge to all of us who have grandchildren.

Let us look specifically at some things that we might do with our grandchildren to help nurture them spiritually. Remember that while some of these things might sound like a simple project that anyone can do with children, they are meant to be done as an occasion to get to know our grandchildren better and to speak to them of God's goodness and love.

Projects to Use If You Live Close to Your Grandchildren

Nature in itself says so much about God and things of the spirit. Many of the things we can do with our grandchildren involve things of nature. Not long ago our grandson Samuel, who was fifteen months old at the time, came to visit us. My husband was holding him as he looked out the kitchen window. Just then a squirrel ran up a tree. Samuel watched it closely and then whispered softly, "Wow." A little later a baby rabbit ran out of a hiding place and sat quietly for a few moments, looking around. Samuel again watched closely and then in a louder whisper said, "Wow!" We want our grandchildren always to see the things that God has created in nature as a "wow!"

We can do some of the following activities (many of them involving nature) together with our grandchildren.

1. Plant a garden and tend it together.
2. Plant an herb garden and see how many ways you can use the herbs.
3. Go to the library and get books on birds. See what kinds of feeders work best for the birds in your area. Either make or buy the feeders and enjoy the birds together.

4. Study the various kinds of butterflies and see how many kinds you can locate in your area.

5. Plant trees together and watch their growth. Care for them during dry seasons and during cold weather.

6. Go fishing together and talk about all the different kinds of fish that God has made.

7. Mark the child's height on a door in your house and periodically see how much he or she has grown.

8. Buy cassettes or compact discs of various kinds of music and help the child learn to recognize various instruments. Use music for times of quiet reflection on God.

9. Exchange something with the children that reminds them of your constant love (for example a small charm that can be carried in their pocket or a locket that they can wear). Let them give you something of theirs in return.

10. When you are together, make up songs or stories about the children or about their parents and sing or tell them to the children.

11. Take quiet "prayer walks" with the children. As they walk quietly, they are to notice things that remind them of God. At the close of the walk, share with each other what you have seen.

12. Study the stars together and help your grandchildren learn the names of the stars and constellations.

If we live far away from our grandchildren, these are some things that we can do with them. Of course, some of the above are also appropriate things to do when visits are made.

1. Send them letters or little notes telling of your love.

2. Send small packages occasionally. Even small things mean a lot to children.

3. Talk to them on the telephone. Send them telephone cards so that they can call you. You might want to get permission from their parents first. Try to remember the details of their conversation, such as their friends' names, what their interests are, and so forth. Refer to these details in later conversations.

4. Send them E-mails or fax letters. I know a man who gets his grandchild's spelling words each week and uses them in his letters.

5. Plan a time for each of you to plant an identical garden, either vegetable or flower. Talk with each other often about how your garden is doing.

6. Audiotape or videotape yourself reading stories to your grandchildren. Send the tape and the book so that they can follow along.

7. Choose a special scripture and share it with your grandchild. Try to find some tangible way to illustrate the verse. For instance, use Isaiah 49:16, "See, I have inscribed you on the palms of my hands." Write each other's initial or name in small letters on your palms. Another scripture might be Psalm 91:4, "He will cover you with his pinions, and under his wings you will find refuge." Each of you might have a small feather to remind you of God's refuge and strength. Matthew 17:20 is another good verse to use, where Jesus says, "For truly I tell you, if you have faith the size of a mustard seed, you will say to this mountain, 'Move from here to there,' and it will move; and nothing will be impossible for you." Give your grandchild a mustard seed (or several) and keep some yourself to remind you to have faith in God.

8. Make a small photograph book with pictures of yourself and send to your grandchildren. Of course, update the pictures from time to time.

9. Have a secret language or code word. Maybe it is about a joke you both think is funny or a code that means, "I love you."

10. Choose a verse of scripture and each of you memorize it. With small children, of course, begin with short phrases and increase the length and difficulty of the material as they mature. The Psalms, for example, contain many wonderful life-giving verses that could easily be learned by heart.

For all our grandchildren, the greatest thing that we can do is pray for them and their parents. We do not know how intercessory prayer works. We do know that when we pray for another, energy is set free and things happen that would not have happened otherwise. And so with confidence we lift our grandchildren to God, asking that God's guidance, protection and strength will be theirs throughout life.

Stephen Bryant, editor and publisher of Upper Room Ministries, says that after his grandfather died, he visited his grandmother. There on his grandfather's chest of drawers was his and his brother's picture. His grandmother told him that each morning as his grandfather dressed, he would say, "Good morning, Steve. Good morning, John." It was his grandfather's way of lifting his grandsons to God every day.

We must find ways to pray consistently and with fervor for our children and grandchildren, doing this in whatever way is best for us. Whether we have our morning devotion at the breakfast table or at a small family altar or by our bed, there should be reminders of those for whom we are praying. We might have pictures of them there, or have their names written on a prayer card or light a candle—anything to remind us that it is our sacred privilege to bring those we love into God's presence.

It is important also for our grandchildren to hear us use their names in prayer. All of us like to be prayed for, and it is especially touching to children to hear their names called in prayer. To know that we are prayed for by those we love is a strengthening thing.

A friend told me a moving story. Her daughter, Laura, was having her fifth birthday. Most of the family had gathered to celebrate it: both sets of grandparents, aunts and uncles. Before the meal, one of her grandfathers gave the blessing. He said something like this: "Oh God, thank you for little girls who are having birthdays today and bless us as we celebrate together."

After the prayer Laura said rather quietly, "Well, what about the name of that little girl?" No one seemed to hear her. Then she said it louder, this time so that all could hear. "I said, what about the name of that little girl?" Then they all heard and understood. Her grandfather was quick to reassure her, as did others. "Of course that little girl with the birthday is you. That little girl's name is Laura. That's who we were praying for."[9]

In the Book of Isaiah we read "Do not fear, for I have redeemed you; I have called you by name, you are mine" (Isa. 43:1). It is reassuring to know that when our names are called in prayer, God knows our names and loves us with an everlasting love. This is important knowledge that we can impart to our grandchildren.

I have one final thought concerning grandparenting: We must remember that we are models for our grandchildren. They see and hear everything we do and often model their behavior from ours. This might boost our ego a bit; but it is also a scary thing and an awesome responsibility.

At a workshop not long ago, a man told me this story. He lived a long distance from his grandson, but made a great effort to see him often. On his recent visit, the little boy was waiting at the window for him, as always. After they greeted each other, the little boy noticed that his grandfather had on a baseball cap. The little boy ran quickly to his room and got his own cap and put it on.

Then they sat down together in a rocking chair with the grandfather holding his grandson. The grandfather's feet were tired after his long trip, so he reached down and untied his shoes and took them off. Then he set them neatly, side by side, beside the chair. The little boy observed this, and then he too untied his shoes, took them off and set them neatly beside his grandfather's. The grandfather said that he realized at that moment how important his presence was to his grandchild and how his life must always reflect the life that he wanted his grandson to emulate. We truly say more to our grandchildren by what we do and how we live than by the words we speak.

In Psalm 71:17–18 we read:

> O God, from my youth you have taught me,
> and I still proclaim your wondrous deeds.
> So even to old age and gray hairs,
> O God, do not forsake me,
> until I proclaim your might
> to all the generations to come.

This is our challenge as grandparents. To tell of God's steadfast love and God's wondrous deeds to the generations to come is not only our challenge, it is our sacred responsibility.

Chapter Five

———

Partners with God

If any of you is lacking in wisdom, ask God, who gives to all generously and ungrudgingly, and it will be given you. But ask in faith, never doubting, for the one who doubts is like a wave of the sea, driven and tossed by the wind....

—James 1:5-6

God's Wisdom

We would all agree, I believe, that it is only by God's wisdom and strength that we are able to parent our children. Many parents have said to me that after they had their children, they realized how ill-prepared they were for parenthood. They came to the task with little understanding and with misguided conceptions about the magnitude of this sacred role.

It is strange that we spend a great deal of time adequately preparing ourselves for so many other things in life—jobs, sports events, volunteer positions, vacations, and trips. But somehow society assumes people know how to parent; therefore no preparation is necessary. Consequently most of us have felt overwhelmed with the task; but with God's help, strength, and wisdom, and often by trial and error, we have done our best. No parent is ever perfect, nor should we try to be. It is only as we see our children and ourselves as pilgrims together on the journey of life that we can live and help our children live life to the fullest.

When you think of being a spiritual guide to your children, you may feel as unprepared for this task as you did for parenting them when they were born. This may be a new role for you, and you may feel apprehensive and unsure of yourself. But just as you learned parenting skills as you went along, you will learn, with God's help, to be a spiritual guide for your children. It takes time, energy, and prayer for God's guidance. But if we are intentional about doing it, we will, with the guidance of the Holy Spirit, find a way to guide our children spiritually. In faith we seek God's guidance, believing that God gives generously and ungrudgingly to those who ask.

Wisdom from Parents Who Are Intentional about Being Spiritual Guides

I believe it helps to look at what parents who are intentional in being a spiritual guide for their children have to say about their experience. As I met with parents and grandparents, I talked with them concerning some of the challenges they face as families and learned of ways in which they are attempting to live faithfully in and through these challenges. We also discussed specific choices they are making that enable them to serve intentionally as spiritual guides to their children or grandchildren. Some of their responses have been discussed in earlier chapters, but I believe their words of wisdom offer illustrations and glimpses of the realities of spiritual parenting. It is helpful to hear from those who are already on the journey, as their stories can speak to our experience and offer strength and encouragement to us as we venture forward.

Thoughts on the Innate Spirituality of Children

Laurie, a mother of two boys, said, "I really believe that children have an innate spirituality. Their incredible innocence and trust speaks to me of God. They believe that God is in control of everything in the world. Their connection with God makes it natural for their minds to turn to God."

Randy, a father of three children, answered, "I definitely believe that children are born with a connection to God. It is as if God has put his fingerprint on them and they are his. It is like the verse says, 'See, I have inscribed you on the palms of my hands' (Isa. 49:16). God loves them, has claimed them, and will never let them go."

Geneen, a mother of a boy and a girl, remarked, "I believe that every child is born with a connection with God. They have that potential. But that potential must be nurtured and nourished and fed. I guess their spiritual growth all depends on what we as parents do with what was there in the first place."

Rena, a Navajo mother, grandmother and educator, said that she felt that children definitely have an innate spirituality. She continued, "In Navajo life when a child is born we believe that they are endowed with all the gifts that they need. The Creator has given them all of these. I know that some child psychologists like Jean Piaget say differently, but we believe that children are born with every possibility. We just have to draw it out of them. We don't have to wait for a certain age or stage."

Thoughts about the Most Difficult Challenges in Parenting

Laurie felt that probably the difficulties in parenting vary depending on the individual parent. For her, one of her greatest challenges is to maintain a sense of balance and hope when she sees all that is going on in the world around her. "I don't want to pass a sense of helplessness and hopelessness on to the kids. I want them to know that God is still here and doing beautiful things. I think, though, that it is becoming more and more difficult to keep negative influences out of our children's lives. Even with their little friends, negative things are brought up. I'd just like to know what they are, though, so that I can explain it and help my children understand it from my perspective."

Randy said that everything about society puts him on the defensive as a parent. "Everything seems to be working against the family and the things we really want to teach our kids. The culture is so fast and our children are dealing with so many things that we don't understand. We can't parent as well when we are on the defensive. This is hard for me and I just wish that I didn't have to be on the defensive all the time."

Geneen said that the most difficult thing she has to face as a parent is to remember to seek constantly what God wants her to do and to try to do that. "We get so rushed and we run out of time. We want to learn to parent in a godly way, but we don't always seek God's guidance on how to do it."

Child psychiatrist Joe Horrigan says that one of the biggest issues today in parenting and one of the most problematic is that children are exposed to too much information at too early an age. He also feels that the expectations parents have for children are out of control in certain segments of society. Their high expectations often contribute to problems such as depression and suicide. "The single most important issue is the time famine that parents experience. There just isn't enough time and everyone is starved: kids and adults. Children are being malnourished when it comes to time and attention from their parents and from important relationships. Consequently they don't have the role modeling with real values which we had one or two generations ago."[1]

Thoughts on the Negative Forces in Society

Do negative societal influences affect parents' endeavors to rear children in the Christian way of life? Many persons with whom I posed this question believe so. Some of their answers, which are similar to those negative forces listed in chapter 2, include the following:

- devaluation of the family, which gives permission to others to do our parenting for us;[2]
- television and the media that permeates all of our lives;
- society in general;
- the "what's best for me" attitude;
- instant gratification;
- the "whatever" (anything goes) syndrome;
- the fast-paced society (hard to hear God when you are running);
- the drug culture; and
- no safe space for children.

In speaking again with Rena, she revealed that some of the forces in society that are impacting Navajo children and youth are unique to their culture. Yet some of these factors speak to the dominant society as well. Rena had this to say:

> We Navajos are caught between two worlds. We are in danger of losing our language and when language is lost, there is no culture. I guess I will have to say that the force in society that is hardest to deal with for my people is economics. We have to struggle to find jobs and often have to move away from our extended family in order to find them. This mobility brings about language loss and loss of values. If children do not live around their aunts, uncles and other relatives, how are they going to learn the values that are so important for us? How are they going to learn

111

to properly address their elders? How will they learn to extend greetings to the family? It used to be that all the family lived close by each other but now everyone has moved away.

Certainly mobility, which separates families and brings a sense of dislocation, is an issue that impacts all of society. The loss of values in families is another issue that touches all of our lives. The parent who mentioned "the whatever syndrome" addressed this issue. This mother said that there is a subtle way of thinking in our society that there is no right or wrong—everything is shaded. She felt that there are some things that are wrong, things that are not part of God's plan for us, and children need to know this.

The parent who talked about the "what's best for me attitude" is aware that this attitude is detrimental to the spiritual lives of children and to our own spiritual lives. To seek always what is best for ourselves or to foster that idea in children is certainly not the way Jesus taught us. "The one who is greatest among you is the servant of all," he said. Children need to find that true happiness comes in doing for others.

One force in society that troubles concerned parents is the strong emphasis on overscheduling children's lives. "They are just too busy, just as we adults are," they said.

It was interesting to hear Laurie's remarks about this issue. She felt strongly that parents today combat a societal pressure to involve their children in multiple activities. Busyness seems to be a valued way of life! "Children come home from day care and go to T-ball, piano lessons, ballet lessons, swimming lessons, and so forth. If they are not involved in various activities, a parent is almost labeled as a neglectful parent. It seems to be a social norm to schedule your kids for this or that."

"It seems that we entertain our children too much and do not feel that we can be with our children without having something scheduled for them to do. We do not want them to be bored, I guess. Yet I think that out of boredom comes creative things. I remember times when my son John was bored; he decided to read a book by himself or had the idea of making a ship out of his building blocks. Being bored, or having time on their hands is not bad for children. It is then that they have time to ponder and ask questions about God. But it seems that we have packed stimulation after stimulation into their lives so that it takes more and more to satisfy them. What is wrong with having a little unscheduled time?"

This is a thought-provoking question and one that is important as we seek to nurture our children spiritually. It is out of solitude and silence that we hear the voice of God. Elijah was listening for the voice of God, and God told him to go out and stand on the mountain, for the Lord was about to pass by.

> Now there was a great wind, so strong that it was splitting mountains and breaking rocks in pieces before the LORD, but the LORD was not in the wind; and after the wind an earthquake, but the LORD was not in the earthquake; and after the earthquake a fire, but the LORD was not in the fire; and after the fire a sound of sheer silence.
>
> —1 Kings 19:11-12

It was in the sound of sheer silence that Elijah heard the voice of God.

Dr. Horrigan believes that there is a strong tendency for parents to overinvolve their children in too many activities at too early an age. This might be piano lessons, French lessons, soccer teams, and so forth. He says that he is dismayed to find that children's schedules are as heavily booked as their parents': "This takes time away from important relationships with Mom and Dad. This overscheduling brings on an empty feeling. Children's lives are filled with 'stuff' and it is not necessarily meaningful 'stuff.' The sense of emptiness that comes from our frenetic pace is a critical issue behind a lot of the problems that we are seeing these days."[3]

How badly we need some of the "sheer silence" that Elijah heard! How badly our children need it if they are to be nurtured in the spiritual life. Without silence and solitude, spiritual growth is just not possible.

Parents' Comments on How They Are Being Spiritual Guides to Their Children

One parent, Laurie, made these comments:

> I am trying to be a spiritual guide for my children. We read Bible stories to them at night and pray together before they go to bed. But also I try to use other times to talk about God and to pray. For instance, when we are in the van and hear a siren, we pray for the person who may be having a problem.
>
> Then we talk about things as they come up daily and discuss how God works in all of life. Of course, when they are scared or nervous, I use these times to talk about how God takes care of us. Sometimes when we are having a hard day, I just scoop one of the boys up and ask God to help me have enough patience for the moment! I think that it is important for them to know that I ask God for help, too.
>
> One thing that I think is important, and I need to do more of this, is to let the boys see me reading my Bible. I try to have a short devotion every day, but some days it's hard. They need to know, though, that I find strength in God's word.

Rena said that she is the firstborn in her family. Because her father is getting old, he has said to her, "You are the oldest. You need to take the responsibility and lead now." Rena says that she is seen as the leader and is asked to lead in prayer at all of their family gatherings. "We don't eat until Grandma

Rena prays! The children know this and they have respect for it. They know not to eat until a prayer is said. In our culture all life is integrated. Spirituality is a part of our daily life and we have a holistic approach to life. Our philosophy is that life is a whole unit and there is no fragmentation."

Dorothy, who is an African American grandmother with the primary responsibility of caring for two of her grandchildren, said that she believes it is very important to keep the children in Sunday school and church. "I say to them, 'Granny's not giving you a choice. This is what we do.' I am the adult and they are the children and I know what is best for them. The children each say a Bible verse and grace at meals. When we say prayers at night before they go to bed, they pray and I do too. If I get busy or forget, they say, 'Come on, Granny, we need to say our prayers.'"

Randy mentioned an interesting point when he said that each child is unique, and he finds that he has to be a spiritual guide to his three children in different ways.

> I wish there could be a 1-2-3 way of doing spiritual guidance, but it doesn't work that way for me. You can get discouraged if you try to do the same thing for each child. If I try to get them together and say, "okay, it's time for devotions, they just roll their eyes." So I have to sneak up on it, so to speak.
>
> For my son, when we are on the way to a ball game or to golf, we read his youth Bible and talk about spiritual things. With my older daughter, I find that early in the morning before she gets out of bed, I can read a verse of scripture to her and talk about things of God. With my younger daughter, I find just the right time to discuss a Bible verse and pray.
>
> Once or twice a week during the dinner hour, we try to talk about what is going on in the world and discuss how God is still present and active in our lives. I just have to remember to pick my spots or

times and not to preach! If I do, a wall comes up and that's the end of it.

Geneen said that for her, being a spiritual guide for her two children meant, first of all, keeping in touch with God herself. She is in a small group that meets weekly to pray for their children. "In fact," Geneen said, "we try to surround our children in prayer. I think it is so important to constantly pray for our children." She continued, "Of course, we use the traditional times of prayer, too, like mealtimes and bedtime. And we pray a lot in the car. In fact this is my favorite time to pray. I used to be shy about praying out loud, but now I just pray out loud in front of the kids in the car. Our children also learn a scripture passage each week and we talk about what they are learning."

Ways That Parents Can Grow Spiritually

Dr. Horrigan contends that if parents lack their own grounding, they are not able to give appropriate grounding to their children. Many adults are trying to find meaning in life, he says. They are asking the question, "What is it all about?" In the recent past, Dr. Horrigan reflects, people were attending church less and less. A change is occurring in that some people are beginning to come back to the church, which reveals that adults are searching for a foundation in life.[4]

Laurie was honest when she said that she realized that often it was easier for her to read about the Bible than to read the Bible itself. She is working on this and is trying to read the Bible more:

> I think that you have to push yourself more and get outside your comfort zone a little. I'm also in a women's prayer support group and that means a lot to me.

Then Randy shared:

> I've found a new way to read the Bible that helps me a lot. It is from Madame Guyon, a seventeenth century spiritual guide. She says to take only one small piece of scripture and work with that for a week or so. She says to "chew" on a phrase or two of one verse for a period of time. This has been a great help to me. I can't digest all the Bible at once, but I can take a small portion and really work with that and see how God is speaking to me through that small portion.
>
> I'm in a small group that meets for two hours weekly and this is a strength to me. Of course, I'm active in a local church. I think that it's so important for my family to be a part of an extended family of Christians. You can learn so much just by being in the presence of others who are on the journey of faith.

Geneen said that Bible study and being in a small group of mothers are two ways she is trying to grow in her spiritual life. "I want to broaden some of the spiritual disciplines that I use and begin to journal. I even want to try fasting for my children, but I haven't started that yet. I think to try some new things would help me tremendously."

Thoughts on Parents' Hopes for Their Children

It was interesting to hear from different parents what they hope for their children. Not one of them said that they wanted their children to be successful. Not one of them said that they wanted them to be affluent. The aspirations they hold for their children are profound. Some of the hopes they listed are that

- they will grow up to love God;
- they will use the gifts and talents that God has given them to give back to the world;

- they will know they are not here by chance—that God has a plan for their lives, loves them unconditionally, and will never forsake them;
- their foundation will be solid enough so that nothing in the world will shake them;
- they will love people well;
- they will have integrity and stand up for what is right;
- they will be thinkers and not go along with what everyone else is doing just because others are doing it;
- they will be productive human beings; and
- they will stay in church and lead a Christian life.

These are heartfelt dreams for children today. With God's wisdom we should strive to make those dreams a reality for every child.

Advice from Parents on How to Be Spiritual Guides

Geneen said that her best advice to parents who want to be spiritual guides for their children is that they pray for and with their children often:

My favorite verse is Lamentations 2:19: "…Pour out your heart like water before the presence of the LORD! Lift your hands to Him for the lives of your children…." This verse is sort of my "theme verse." I think it would be a good one for all parents. I often go back in the children's rooms at night after they are asleep and have a prayer. As I touch them gently, I ask God to guide their lives. Also I would advise parents to ask God for wisdom on how to parent and how to sift through all the worldly stuff. It is important too to ask God's help on how to avoid the "Frantic Family Syndrome." We are all just too busy.

My best advice to parents who are earnestly seeking to guide their children spiritually would be to

pray with and for them. I think too that it is important for them to pray about decisions regarding the
family—not to just go with the flow. Even if your
neighbors are doing a certain thing, that doesn't mean
that is right for your children. Seek God's guidance,
even in the little things.

Randy said that his best advice to other parents was that
they not be afraid to admit that they had made a mistake or
that they were not perfect. "I think that our children need to
see that sometimes we are inadequate as parents and that
sometimes our faith is inadequate. When we make a mistake,
it's best to say to our children, 'I blew it.' Guiding our children spiritually is not about our being perfect. In fact, it's not
about us anyway. It's about God who loves us just as we are,
not as we should be. I think God is saying to us, 'I love you as
you are. You don't have to change, grow or be good, because
my love is unconditional.' If we can just get this message
across to our children, we will have done a good thing."

Dr. Horrigan says when parenting, we should take seriously our role by using common sense about what kids need
and about the amount of time and attention they need. He
gives some practical advice for parents: turn off the television,
don't have cable television, use the VCR for videos approved
by parents and most important, spend time one-on-one with
your children. He also says we should teach children the
basics of right and wrong, conferring a sense that there is
meaning to what goes on in the world and that there is a
God who sits behind it all.[5]

Wisdom from Grandparents

Listening to grandparents talk about their grandchildren is
always interesting. They have wisdom not only from their life
experiences but also from having reared their own children.
Their perspective is deeper and broader and as one grandmother put it, "It's a lot easier for us to see past the small stuff

to the things that are important in life. With our grandchildren, there is not the pressure that we had with our own children and there is no guilt." The following comments are some nuggets of wisdom gleaned from conversations with a group of grandparents.

Thoughts on the main role of grandparenting include to:

- fill in the spots that parents do not have time or resources for;
- be the glue that holds the family together;
- be the ones to pass on the traditions of the family, to be the link with the past;
- guide our family in upholding the values we deem important;
- affirm church attendance as being extremely important and not be afraid to ask children or grandchildren if they attended church the previous Sunday;
- be a spiritual guide to our grandchildren by letting them see us reading our Bibles and praying and by teaching them to do these things;
- ensure that grandchildren understand what the traditions of the church mean; such as the real meaning of Christmas and Easter;
- provide a lot of love for the grandchildren and teach them love for others;
- be a role model or important figure in grandchildren's lives; and
- give advice when it is asked for but if not, to be silent.

How to Be a Spiritual Guide to Grandchildren

Carrie felt that one of the ways that she is a spiritual guide to her grandchildren is by using nature to emphasize how God has created everything in world. She goes on walks with them and looks for leaves and other pretty things that speak of God's creation. She takes them to the creek and lets the children look for interesting things. "One of our favorite things to do is to take an old milk carton, cut out one end and put cellophane across the bottom. Then the children can push the carton to the bottom of the water and see what is there. They love to do this," she said.

Dody said that one way she is being a spiritual guide is by singing with her grandchild. "If she is staying with me, we sing and sing, even after we are in bed at night. I teach her to sing the Doxology and other songs of faith. I want her to know these life-giving words of faith. I also teach her the Lord's Prayer and the Apostle's Creed, even though she is too young to understand the words. She will understand them someday."

"You know, maybe one of the best things that I do, or try to do," Jean said, "is to be patient with my grandchildren. I may be the only patient person they encounter today. Everyone is so rushed."

Rachel remarked that one of the ways she is trying to be a spiritual guide for her grandchildren is by reading to them. She finds books that contain values she wants to instill in them. By reading these books to them, she hopes these values will become a part of their lives. The group agreed, saying that it is best not to be "preachy" and that slipping things in "on the children's blind side" is often the best tactic.

Zena gave examples of several things she had done with her grandchildren. She said she sometimes sends them a postcard, writing a verse of scripture in a circle, and leaving one or two of the words out. She includes the Bible reference so that the child can look it up. Also, if she is aware that one of her grandchildren is going through some difficult time, she writes the child a note every day for five days. Sometimes she even sends a little secret surprise in the mail every day for five days. These are two ways that she can surround a grandchild with a little concentrated love.

Other helpful comments by the group were:

- LaJune said she found it meaningful to help her grandchild make gifts for their parents and for shut-ins. "This is a good way to teach them to show compassion," she said.
- Zena said she felt that just listening to grandchildren as they talk is so important. "We have the time to listen and it's so important to let them talk about things that are important to them without interrupting."
- JoAnn said she enjoys teaching her children some of the old games she used to play. "They don't learn these anywhere else," she said. Dusk is a magical time for children and there are a lot of games that can be played then, such as hide and seek.
- Someone mentioned that it is good from time to time for the grandparent to say, "Tell me your memories." That often opens deeper conversation.
- The group agreed that it is very important to keep up with and to attend special events if possible— grandparent's day at school, recitals, ball games.
- Someone mentioned that one of the hardest things to do if there is a divorce involving your son or daughter is to watch what is said to the grandchildren about the other parent. One grandmother said she tried to abide by the old maxim, "If you can't say anything good, don't say anything at all."

In speaking of discipline and their grandchildren, all agreed that if the parents were present with their children, discipline was the parent's job. Yet they all felt that grandchildren need to abide by the rules that grandparents set while they are with them. "It is all right to love them, even spoil them," they said, "but we are the adults and they are the children. It's not about letting them think that anything goes. There are limits and they need to know the rules and limits for their behavior. It's all right for us to say that food should not be taken into the living room or that there is to be no running in the house."

Can God Speak to Children at Any Age or Stage?

There was consensus in the group that God can speak to children at any age. One person said, "We cannot limit God." Dorothy, who was quoted in an earlier section, said, "Of course God can speak to children. God made them, so God can talk to them whenever God wants!"

Rena had an interesting point. "I believe that the Creator can speak through children as well as speak to children. Out of the mouths of babes wisdom comes! God has his own way of speaking to children," she said.

Do Children Have an Innate Spirituality?

All of the grandparents in the group shared some experience with a grandchild that caused them to believe that children do, indeed, have an innate spirituality. Many of those present stated that this spirituality was not something that had been taught the child. They spoke of the children insisting on praying, many of them wanting to hold hands as they prayed. They talked about the sense of innate wonder that their grandchildren have.

Carrie told about her own three-year-old daughter, Elizabeth, who went for a walk with her in the early spring. Although there was still snow on the ground, a beautiful crocus had dared to push its head through the snow toward the bright sunlight. Elizabeth ran to the flower, knelt down beside it, and cupped her little hands around the flower. "Dear God," she prayed aloud, "thank you for the sun and rain that make the flowers grow." Our group was moved by her story. Children often touch us with their spirituality!

Grandparents—Especially Grandmothers— Are the "Kin Keepers" of Society

The grandmothers I spoke with all felt that grandmothers are probably the "kin keepers" of society. "We are the ones who call the brood together," they said. "We do the cooking and organizing. We are the ones to remember birthdays and other holidays. We are the ones to plan family reunions."

Mary told about her granddaughter, Krista, who at first resisted going to a family reunion with Mary and her husband. "Now she wouldn't miss it for the world. She knows that she has a lot of aunts, uncles, and cousins, and she loves seeing all of them." Mary has given Krista a great gift of knowing her extended family, which is so important to children.

When I asked Dorothy if she thought that grandmothers were the "kin keepers" of society, she remarked, "I don't think, I *know* that's true. When anyone has a problem, they come to me. I don't interfere in their problems unless they ask me, but I am the leader of the family and they come to me often. Every holiday is celebrated at my house—birthdays, Easter, Christmas. They all bring food but it is always at my house. In the African American tradition, everyone looks to the grandmother to be the one who holds the family together."

Those of us who are grandparents have a great opportunity to impact the lives of our grandchildren. The role that we play depends on us. It is hoped that we will choose to be a part of their lives, being active participants and intermingling our lives with theirs.

Dr. Horrigan comments, "I think one of the real pities of the contemporary American society is that we have often marginalized older Americans and haven't encouraged them to maintain connections with their family. Parents frequently become so consumed with their own lifestyles and issues that they fail to put appropriate time and attention into integrating their own parents into the lives of their children and families."[6]

When grandparents are not involved in the lives of their grandchildren, everyone misses out. Grandparents can find so much joy in sharing in the lives of grandchildren, and grandchildren can be enriched beyond measure from their grandparents' lives and experiences. We need to take hold of this precious opportunity and use it to the utmost. In talking with one grandfather, he said, "Grandchildren are just great, but try not to have more than one new one born a year." When I asked him why, Jerry said, "Well, they last longer that way!" Most of us want them to last as long as possible.

Words of Wisdom on Trauma in Parenting

As has been said earlier, it is not realistic to think that just because we have decided to seek a deeper spiritual life or to be a spiritual guide for our children that life will become problem free. Anyone who has been intentional about living a spiritual life will tell us that this is just not the case. To enter into being a spiritual guide with this misconception will bring disappointment and disillusionment.

Several parents who have had to deal with some trauma, disappointment or discouragement in parenting were gracious enough to tell their stories. They do this with the hope that their story might be beneficial to others who are going through a difficult time.

Hank's Story

Hank began his story by telling a little bit of his background. He had had loving parents and he and his siblings remembered their childhood with happiness and appreciation. When Hank married and had children of his own, he assumed they would have the same kind of childhood that he did. But times had changed and life now seemed more hectic and less secure. Hank's work caused the family to move several times and these disruptions took its toll on his children.

As the children grew, it was soon apparent that something was wrong with his oldest son. The boy became such a behavioral problem that he disrupted the whole family, shattering any dream of a peaceful home life for the family. Finally it became evident that the boy was suffering from an emotional illness.

At first Hank denied that anything was wrong, choosing instead to think that his son was just going through a difficult stage. When the evidence was too apparent to ignore, Hank sought medical guidance for his son. Nothing seemed to help and the whole family suffered terribly because of the illness of one of its members.

The teenage years were extremely difficult and stretched the family almost to the breaking point. Hank and his wife worked together and held on through the storms that seemed to hit the family in waves. Finally, in young adulthood, their son seemed for a time to get better, met and married a young woman, and moved away from the family. Gradually he distanced himself from the family, finally refusing to communicate with them or to see them at all.

When I asked Hank if there was a stage in his life that he blamed God for this misfortune, he said, "There is a prayer of thanksgiving that my wife and I use every day. Part of it goes like this:

New every morning is your love for us,
　　Great God of Light,
and all day long you are working for good
　　in the world.

If I truly pray this prayer and believe that God is working for good in the world, how could I be angry or blame God for this event? I believe that God is working for my best good; God is not a God who imposes hardships on God's children.

I could say, though, that at one time I did blame circumstances or situations that may have brought this about. My wife and I even blamed ourselves, wondering what we had done wrong. But I didn't blame God. I finally have come to the place where I can leave my son in God's hands and say, 'I've done all I can do, God. Please take care of him now.' My faith and my wife's faith in a loving God has been the thing that has carried us through.

Alice's Story

Alice and her husband had wanted a child for a long time. Finally after years of marriage, they had a daughter. Paula was the delight of their lives, and they thanked God for her daily. After Alice's husband death, she found much comfort in her daughter. Paula eventually married and had three beautiful children.

They lived close enough so that Alice was very active in the lives of Paula and her children. Alice kept them often and delighted in doing so. One Sunday she kept them all day so that Paula and her husband could get away on a short day-trip.

That night after Paula returned, everything seemed normal. She put the children to bed and she and her husband went to bed. Later that night Paula died suddenly and unexpectedly.

When I asked Alice how she felt about God at this point and if she wondered where God was in all of this, she said, "As far as I know, God has never made a mistake. God has blessed my life in so many beautiful ways. Just because this has happened, I can't turn against God and blame God now."

In describing how she got through the initial shock and grief of losing her only child, Alice said, "I couldn't have made it without my faith. Two passages of scripture have really sustained me. 'Do not let your hearts be troubled. Believe in God, believe also in me' (John 14:1), and 'We know that all things work together for good for those who love God, who are called according to his purpose' (Rom. 8:28). These passages have helped me so much."

I asked Alice what she felt her role was in her grandchildren's lives now. She answered, "I want to help their daddy in any way I can without intruding. I would never want to do that. But I can help him by picking them up after school and keeping them until he gets home from work. I want to help them appreciate all that their mother taught them—to pray, to respect and help others, to love God. And I want to help them know that they will see their mother again in the life to come."

Penny's Story

Scott was born six weeks prematurely to Penny and Steve. Their little girl was two years old at the time. At first they and the doctors believed that developmentally, Scott was just slow because of being premature. But gradually Penny began to suspect something was wrong, and at eighteen months Scott was diagnosed with cerebral palsy. He learned to walk at two years of age and had his first surgery then. He has had eight surgeries in all, mostly on his legs. He has also had a hernia repair and later eye surgery.

When they first received the diagnosis of cerebral palsy, Penny said that her first thought was, "How in the world are we going to do this for the rest of our lives?" They both knew that it would require all of the emotional and physical energy that they could muster, because it would be a constant challenge with very little break for either of them.

When I asked Penny what her thoughts about God were in all of this, she was thoughtful for a time. Then she said that she never, ever felt "Why me?" nor did she wonder why God let this happen. "The strength came because I knew that I had to do it. Scott had many problems early on and needed constant care, so I was too busy to sit around and say, 'Woe is me.' I had to keep going for the children's sake."

The evening after Penny and Steve had been given the diagnosis of Scott's condition, Steve went to a meeting. He happened to sit across from a couple who had a child with a similar condition to Scott's. He and Penny both feel that it was divine providence that Steve "just happened" to sit near them. They shared their own situation with Steve, which helped a great deal. Also, providentially, Penny and Steve have been at the right place to give other young parents a word of encouragement and hope when they have received a similar prognosis about a child.

Penny feels that their faith in God has grown through this experience. In fact, Penny shared, "If it hadn't been for Scott, I might not have spent as much time in prayer and Bible study!" Their friends at church were so supportive in those early years and continue to be a comfort to them.

For many years Steve and Penny organized their lives around what Scott could or could not do. Because he could not go to his own Sunday school class for many years, they kept the two- and three-year-old children in the nursery at their church so Scott could stay with them.

Later on, as Scott was able, they began to go to church and sit together as a family. Now that Scott is older, he enjoys sitting with some of his friends. In order for Scott to have some of same enjoyable activities as other teenagers, Penny and Steve both went on youth mission trips as counselors so that Scott could go and be a part of this enriching experience.

At present Scott is thirty-one and has been approved to enter a custodial home with another boy and a caretaker. He is excited about this and hopes that it works out soon. Penny and Steve feel that he is ready and that this will be an exciting next step for him.

I asked Penny what was the most difficult thing that she had to face as a parent. She said it was the uncertainty of Scott's future. "What is going to happen to him when we are gone?" she asked. When I asked Penny what her hopes for her children are, she said that she hopes they will be loving, productive members of society, their church and their community, and that they will have a feeling of fulfillment in their lives. As parents she and Steve have always worked toward making these hopes viable possibilities in their children's lives.

Mary and Owen's Story

One Wednesday, Mary was in the hospital, having just given birth to a new baby boy, Clark. On Friday her mother Margaret came to see her and the new baby. Owen, her husband, was there too with their three-and-a-half-year-old son, Thomas. After they had visited for awhile, Margaret decided to drive to her home, which was about thirty miles away, to check on an addition that was being built on her house. She would return that same evening. When Thomas heard this, he wanted to go with her because he wanted to get a milkshake at the local drugstore. There was some discussion about whether he should go with Margaret or go home with his dad. Finally the decision was that he should go with his grandmother, so he kissed his parents goodbye and he and Margaret left.

Later in the afternoon, Owen received word that there had been a car accident and both Margaret and Thomas had been injured. Not knowing what to expect and without telling Mary, Owen rushed frantically to the hospital (a different one from where his wife and baby were) where he found out the terrible news. Thomas had been killed instantly in the accident and Margaret was in critical condition.

After taking care of some details and doing what he could there at that hospital, Owen had to go back to the other hospital to tell his wife the devastating news. Mary said that at first when he told her, she was in total denial. She refused to believe it saying, "No, that just can't be," over and over and over again. With time, of course, she realized the truth and the awful grief began.

Owen said that on that first day he had two phrases going around in his head. One was, "What do I do with God in all this?" The other was, "What in the world do I do without God in this? I can't live through this without God." The next morning Owen said that as he awoke, his first thought was, "This day is going to be the worst day of my life because I must go pick out a casket for my little son."

Both Mary and Owen said that they could not have made it without their family and friends. Mary said that she was so grateful for those who were able just to let her talk. "I needed to talk about Thomas," she said. "I am so grateful for those who were able to let me talk and talk and say what I needed to say. Some of those closest to us just couldn't bear to talk about it because they were in such pain themselves." Owen mentioned a friend who came and just stood there beside him. He didn't offer any words of comfort, no platitudes about why this had happened, no theological assumptions—just stood there and was there for him if he needed anything. Mary and Owen said that their baby Clark also was a comfort to them. "It helped immensely to have him fill our empty arms," they said.

Margaret, they were to find out, had a major stroke while driving home that day. This, of course, had caused the wreck. She remained in the intensive care unit for three months and in the hospital a total of seven months, where she had three more strokes. Mary, her sister, and other family members visited Margaret on a regular basis. She eventually left the hospital and has had many good days during these past few years.

Mary and Owen had a third son, Jeff, two years after that fateful day when she was in the hospital with their second son. The two boys are doing well and Mary and Owen have been excellent parents. Owen remarked, "After what happened to Thomas, I want to treasure every moment of my two boys' lives. My advice to parents is to spend a lot of time with their children because it is in those day-to-day encounters that you can speak with them about things of the spirit."

Good Can Come Out of Our Brokenness

Shel Silverstein has a beautiful story called *The Missing Piece.* He tells of a wheel that had a missing pie-shaped piece. It wanted more than anything to be whole, so the wheel went everywhere looking for its missing piece. Because it was not perfectly whole, it had to roll very slowly. The good news was, though, that because it was slow it had time to talk with the flowers and the small animals. It had time to admire the beauty of each day and to encourage those along the way.

One day, to the wheel's great joy, it found the missing piece. After it was inserted in the proper place, the wheel began to roll very fast along the way. This, however, created a different problem. Now there was no time to talk to the flowers and small animals. There was no time to greet others or to enjoy the day.

Finally, exasperated with its new accelerated way of life, the wheel stopped, took out the piece and discarded it. Now it could again bump along at a slower pace and enjoy life and those with whom it came in contact.[7] It found out that to be perfect did not always ensure happiness.

Sometimes we have the mistaken idea that our families should be perfect. We as parents should be perfect—we think—and our children should be perfect. Our lives should be picture perfect. Of course, in our innermost beings, we know that this is not the way life is. But we like to imagine that if "this thing were changed" in our family or if "that thing were different," then life would be perfect.

The truth is that it is most often in our brokenness, our imperfections, that we find God the closest to us. It is when we are struggling with some concern of our own that we are the most compassionate, the most loving with those around us. Miraculously, God takes our situation, just as it is; and if we allow it, God takes us just as we are and transforms us so that we can live life to the fullest.

God takes our heartfelt longings, our unrealistic expectations, and our dreams of being whole and gathers them up and enfolds us in God's loving embrace. Then, in the very midst of our brokenness, we are empowered to become whole. Saint Augustine has said, "...I can find no safe place for my soul except in you. In you may my scattered longings be gathered together, and from you may no part of me ever depart."[8] Only as we are able to pray in this way are we made truly whole. God takes our scattered longings for the restoration of the brokenness in our lives and in the lives of our children and our grandchildren and gathers them up into His loving embrace, healing, soothing, restoring, and making us all whole.

Chapter Six

Our Life Together in God

Some years ago when our oldest granddaughter was two, she and her mother went to the beach with us for a few days. There, next to our motel, was one of the tallest swings I have ever seen. Of course Maggie wanted to try it out but since it was so tall, I was afraid for her to swing alone and took her in my lap. She held on tightly as we began to move back and forth, higher and higher. With her wispy little blond hair blowing in the wind, she began to squeal with delight. Finally she called down to anyone who was within hearing distance, "Look, look, everyone look. I'm running, I'm running."

Maggie's limited vocabulary did not equip her to express what she was experiencing. We had to teach her the word *swinging* so that she could better describe what was happening in her life. The same is true with our children in describing their experiences with God. We must give them a vocabulary of faith so that they can adequately express their encounters with the transcendent. This is one of the roles of spiritual guides of children—to teach them the language of faith.

When I was four years old, I remember vividly having a very moving, religious experience. I was outside playing with a little friend in the late afternoon on a beautiful summer day. Our attention was suddenly riveted on a gorgeous sunset splashed across the sky, displaying magnificent muted colors of purples, pinks, and mauves. We were overwhelmed and speechless, and a feeling welled up within me that I had never experienced before.

Tears began to stream down my face, and about that time my mother called me to come in for supper. As I entered the kitchen where she was preparing the evening meal, she noticed my tear-streaked face. "Why, Betty," she asked, "what is the matter?" Not knowing how to describe my feelings to her, I told her that I had mashed my finger in the door! I believe that many children have similar experiences of intense spiritual depth, and either because they do not have words to express them, or because they are afraid they will not be believed or will be ridiculed, they keep these to themselves.

Marjorie Thompson has said that "children can surprise us with the immediacy of their spiritual perceptions. What they need most from adults are the affirmation and support of those perceptions, the context of religious tradition by which to understand their own experience, and a language with which to express their faith."[1]

What is this vocabulary of faith, this religious language that we are talking about? Jerome Berryman says that "religious language helps us come closer to God and the whole network of self, others, nature, and God. This is a language of mystery." Later he continues, "Religious language, then, is a language of exclamation. If we were to give this language game a name, we might call it 'Wow!'"[2] (Remember my grandson Samuel when he saw the creatures of nature and said "Wow!")

We can give our children many words from our faith, some of which we know they cannot fully comprehend until a later age, but words, nevertheless, that will be helpful to them in expressing their faith. Some of these words or phrases might be *amen, alleluia, praise, grace, mercy, hosanna, steadfast love, child of God, God bless you, Jesus,* and *Holy Spirit.*

Also include various names for God, such as Holy One, Father, Creator, Lord, and Good Shepherd. (For the very young child, however, it is best just to call God "God" because using various names can be confusing.)

It's not that we want to teach children pat answers for every experience. No, what we want to do is to give them words to describe authentically what they have experienced themselves. Of course along the way they will learn some data, some facts, and some theological meanings. But this is not our main goal. Our main goal is to help them describe their own authentic experiences of God.

John Wesley offers advice on this. He says, "I ask you in earnest to think through carefully how you teach your children about the deep things of God. Beware of the common but bad way of making children parrots instead of Christians."[3] We do not want them to parrot our words; we want them to have descriptive words of their own.

We try to give children our faith language, help them as they try to use it, and then we must trust that God will help them grow in it as they go along. It is so important for families to be in church as much as possible, to hear the liturgy, the prayers, the scripture, the sacred stories of fellow pilgrims, and to observe the rituals of our faith. It is by hearing these words over and over again that children internalize them and make them their own.

Marjorie Thompson makes another important point when she says, "The language of faith we offer children needs to include movement, signs, and acts as well as words."[4] She suggests that "concrete forms of expression such as kneeling, bowing, passing the peace, making the sign of the cross, lifting hands in praise or folding them in prayer can be helpful.... [Children] need tangible, visible signs and symbols in order to assimilate the message of faith."[5] As spiritual guides for children we are in a position to offer them opportunities to experience these concrete forms of expression.

In our life together in the family and in the community of faith, children learn our rituals, our traditions, and our language of faith. These are the concrete things that help ground them in the life of faith. This spiritual formation is not something that happens in an instant but continues throughout childhood and throughout life. As pilgrims together with our children, we will have many opportunities for sharing our life in God together.

Children as Spiritual Guides

As stated earlier, often children are spiritual guides for those around them. We tend to tell children "to wait." "Wait until you are older." "Wait until you are taller." "Wait until next summer." Wait, wait, and wait. But children should not have to wait to be authentic and valuable examples of faith for us. They have worth now and should be seen as children of God.

When the children were brought to Jesus, they did not have to wait to see him. In fact, when Jesus realized that the disciples were turning the children away, he was angry with the disciples. "Let the little children come to me," he said. "Do not stop them; for it is to such as these that the kingdom of God belongs." He continued, "Truly I tell you, whoever does not receive the kingdom of God as a little child will never enter it" (Mark 10:13-15).

Imagine that! Jesus said that we must become as little children in order to enter the kingdom of God. That must have sounded to the disciples like a strange requirement for entering the kingdom—to become as a little child. The disciples had recently had a discussion on who was the greatest; now they learn that all they have to do is to become as little children. To be trusting, to be open to God's presence and power, to be sincere in all our dealings, to be pure and holy—these are the things necessary to enter the realm of God.

Those adults who have opportunities to be around children understand why Jesus gave this instruction as a requirement to be eligible for entrance into God's kingdom. We have witnessed children's purity and innocence. We have grown ourselves by sharing in their faith and trust in God. We have marveled at the innate knowledge they have about things of the spirit.

When Alice's daughter, Paula, died (see Alice's story, page 127) several children came to the funeral home since Paula taught preschool. One child came up to my friend Alice, put her arms around her and said, "Don't be sad, Miss Alice, because Miss Paula is with God now. She is an angel in heaven." Without prompting, this child brought a word of comfort to one who was grieving.

Years ago when my children were small, the young son of one of our friends died suddenly several days before Easter. He was the same age as one of our boys, so my heart was heavy for his parents. I knew how we would feel if it had been our son, and my grief for his mother was particularly great, since Eric was their only son. Rather lamely, I'm afraid, I tried to talk to our children about Eric's death.

One morning in the midst of his play, Tim became very quiet. Then he came to me and with a smile on his face and a note of authentic joy in his voice and said, "You know, I bet this is the best Easter Eric has ever had." In my feelings of grief, I did not understand his meaning. "Why is that, Tim?" I asked. "Why because he is with Jesus and God in heaven!" he exclaimed. My child's statement opened the way for our family to have some wonderful discussions on life and death and on heaven and the afterlife. Often children open the way for us to approach things of the spirit.

A friend told me about going to church one day and being overjoyed to see that the baby that her friends had been waiting to adopt had arrived from China. She took her little son Jeff over to meet the little girl. Later, after they returned home, out of the blue five-year-old-Jeff said, "I'm going to go to China someday and tell everybody there about the joy of God." My friend was astounded. They had never used the terminology "joy of God" with Jeff, but this seemed to come from somewhere deep within him, from a spirituality that was there from the beginning.

This same friend shared a moving story about her oldest son, Thomas. When he was three years old, his great-grandmother died. The parents debated whether to take Thomas to the funeral home, but at the last minute decided to take him with them. When he saw his great-grandmother in the casket, he said to those around him, "Granny is not really there. She is in heaven with God and has new bones now." The elderly woman had been in a great deal of pain with arthritis, and this was Thomas's way of saying that she was now whole and pain-free.

My oldest grandchild Maggie has been a guide to me in the area of prayer. We had been visiting in her home, and as we were leaving to go back to our home, she asked me to go with her because she wanted to show me something. I followed her up a hill as she led me through a wooded area near her home. Finally we arrived at a beautiful cleared, circular spot. The ground was covered with luscious green moss, and the area was surrounded by small fernlike trees, as if to wall in the small sanctuary. It was truly a holy place.

We stood there in silence for several minutes. When I asked Maggie what she did there, she said, "Well, I just think or I pray, or I just be quiet. This is my secret place and I don't show it to just anybody." I thanked her for sharing it with me and encouraged her to continue going to her secret place.

As we got in the car to drive away, Maggie handed me a small triangle that she had made out of a sheet of paper. She had started at one end and continued to fold and refold it, until it was a very small triangle. Then she had decorated it with flowers. As she handed it to me she said, "This is something to remember me by. When you pray, hold this in your hand and pray for me."

Maggie taught me that we all need our secret places—places where we feel the presence of God and where we can be silent before our Creator. To have a place where we can think, be silent, and pray to God is so important for our spiritual life. It is in the secret places that we are recreated into the person God has made us to be.

It is important too as Maggie has showed me, for us to have things that remind us of those we love. As parents, grandparents and those with special children in our lives, we need to have tangible things by which to remember our precious children. This might be a picture of each of them placed in our place of prayer. It might be something they have made for us or a picture they have drawn. It might be some memento of our time together with them. Then as we are praying for them, we can hold or look at this special thing that we use to remember them and lift their name to God in prayer.

If Every Child Is Our Child

Matthew begins his Gospel with the birth of Jesus and is the only gospel writer to include the story of the wise men. He tells us that Herod instructed the wise men to go and find the child, and then return and tell him where the infant Jesus could be found. When they did not go back to Herod as he had requested, Herod was furious and had every male child under two years old killed. Then Matthew quotes from the prophet Jeremiah saying:

> A voice was heard in Ramah, wailing and loud lamentation, Rachel weeping for her children; she refused to be consoled, because they are no more.
> —Matthew 2:18

Most often when we think of children we think of our own children. We think of our grandchildren, the children we know at church, and the children in our community. But there are many other children in the world, children who are at risk because of poor health care, poverty, abuse, wars, and neglect. These are the ones for whom we should weep without consolation.

If we truly want to be disciples of Jesus, we must have concern for all the children of the world. We learned the words to this song long ago, "Jesus loves the little children of the world." The song goes on to say that they are all precious in his sight. If they are precious to Jesus, they must be precious to us too.

If all children were our children, what would we do for them? We know what we would do. We would see that they have enough to eat. We would see that they have proper health care. We would see that they have a comfortable place to live. We would protect them from those things that are harmful to them. And we would love them unconditionally.

How can I do this, we ask? There are so many children in need out there. They live so far away. They have so many needs for which I can not provide. While it is true that some of them live far away, it is also true that some of these children live in our own communities, our own neighborhoods, our own towns. And while we cannot help all of the children everywhere, we can help some of the children somewhere. "Truly, I tell you, just as you did it to one of the least of these who are members of my family, you did it to me," Jesus says to us (Matt. 25:40).

All of us have the talents and the means to be of help to children in some way. We just have to look deep within ourselves to find what it is that we are capable of doing. Even if we are deeply involved with our own children or our grandchildren, we must—to save the at-risk children of the world—be willing to go the extra mile and help some of the children whom no one else cares for or loves.

If you think that there is absolutely nothing you can do for children, let me share a few suggestions. Many of these children never come through the doors of our churches, but some of them do. Even if we do not have children of our own or grandchildren, we can extend God's love and affirmation to the children with whom we come in contact. The church provides us with a community within which we can be grandparents to many children.

One grandfatherly man I know spotted a little boy who came to his church. It was obvious that the boy was neglected and was developing some behavior problems. The man took the little boy as his own particular challenge. He sought him out each Sunday, hugged him, and brought him small gifts of love. And he told the little boy that he loved him and was proud of him. His favorite saying to the little boy was, "Hey, you know what? You are a great kid!"

Gradually, the little boy changed. He smiled more. His behavior began to change for the better. He held his shoulders up and his head high. He had a friend who loved him, and this made all the difference. This is the sort of thing that we can all do for children, whether they are in our church, our neighborhood, or our community.

I know a woman who has a large farm with horses. Her children are grown now, but she still keeps the horses because she loves them. Not long ago she decided that there was something that she should be doing with her horses, so she began a program that she calls "Horse Play." She invites children who are mentally and physically challenged to come to her farm and ride the horses. This project has become a ministry for her and has made a great deal of difference in the lives of many children.

I have had the joy of being involved in a church that has a strong tutoring program for children who live in marginalized circumstances. Members of the church volunteer their time by going weekly to a church in the children's neighborhood and tutoring the children one-on-one for several months. The number of children that this program has helped is unknown. Yet, by faithfully giving of their time, these tutors have instilled self-confidence, have increased the children's skills, and have given hope for the future to countless numbers of children. Needless to say, the church volunteers have been blessed in this ministry themselves.

A young father I know has three beautiful sons. In addition to doing an excellent job of fathering his own sons, he finds time to work with persons who are physically and mentally challenged. Mark has excelled in weight lifting and feels that one contribution he can make is to help others learn this skill. It is important to him to offer this training to those who otherwise might not have the opportunity to learn. Often his students are involved in sports events in other locations and Mark goes with them as their coach, instructing, encouraging, and assuring them of their self-worth.

I remember with affection my friend LaDonna who had worked with children all of her life. After she had spent some time in retirement, she became blind. This was very difficult for her because she had always been a giving person, a person always helping others. She did not let her blindness stop her from reaching out to children, however. Her friends gave her the yarn they had left over after knitting some project, and she took those scraps and knitted them into small stocking caps for children. This gave her much joy because she felt that she was still meeting the needs of children.

If every child is our child, how dare we say "there is nothing I can do for needy children"? There is something you, and only you, can do; but it will require your time, your patience, your perseverance, and your commitment. Jesus said, "Whoever welcomes one such child in my name welcomes me, and whoever welcomes me welcomes not me but the one who sent me"(Mark 9:37). Surely we want to be a part of welcoming the children whom Jesus cherished.

Hope That Does Not Disappoint Us

An important role of the spiritual guide, I believe, is to instill hope. I have mentioned hope briefly in another chapter but because it seems to me that hope is a commodity that is drastically lacking in our world today, I want to mention it again. As adults we often let the daily news of our country and the world discourage us. We hear of wars and rumors of wars, and fears abound. We see flashed before our eyes vivid pictures of people who are being displaced from their homes throughout the world, and a sense of dread sets in. We hear of crime that begins in our own neighborhoods and stretches across the globe, and terror fills our hearts. Where is God in all of this, we wonder, sometimes aloud and sometimes in the secret recesses of our hearts. Our lack of hope spills over into the hearts of our children, because we cannot give to them what we do not have ourselves.

The writer of the Book of Lamentations talks of God's mercies. As he remembers all that God has already done he concludes,

> But this I call to mind and therefore I have hope:
> The steadfast love of the LORD never ceases,
> His mercies never come to an end;
> they are new every morning;
> great is your faithfulness.
> "The LORD is my portion," says my soul,
> "therefore I will hope in him."
> —Lamentations 3:21-24

I know I have used this scripture in another chapter, but these are powerful words that have sustained me and held me steady during times of doubt, sadness, fear, and despair.

"Therefore I will hope in him." It is this hope we must transfer to our children: hope in a faithful God who will never leave us nor forsake us; hope in the knowledge that God's goodness will prevail; hope that a new day is coming when all evil, sin, and pain will be overcome. Hope is the antidote for the meaninglessness and despair that we see among our children today. Studies have shown that meaninglessness and despair are not consigned to any one socioeconomic group of children. These soul-robbing realities are found in children from wealthy homes as well as in children living in poverty.

When children learn to trust expectantly in a God who is in control of this world, they will find zest for living. Swiss theologian Emil Bruner has said, "What oxygen is to the lungs, such is hope to the meaning of life."[6] This hope is what our children and our world are hungry for. Brazilian theologian Rubem A. Alves has said that "hope is hearing the melody of the future."[7] This is the tonic that strengthens the souls of children as they face the uncertainties of the future.

As spiritual guides for our children, we must help them fill the hunger for God that is within them. In the words of Saint Augustine of Hippo, "You have made us for yourself, and our hearts are restless till they find their rest in you."[8]

One writer has suggested that "this materialistic age has clouded [our] spiritual eyes until [we] no longer ask the great human questions every generation has asked: Who am I? What is the meaning of my life? Where is truth? How can I know God?" He continues by asking, "Can it be that our technological civilization is so absorbed in tangible realities that spiritual realities are crowded out?"[9] When we fail to fill that hunger for God with things of the spirit, the hunger will be filled with something else—often something that is detrimental to our souls.

Paul in his letter to the Romans has a beautiful blessing for the people: "May the God of hope fill you with all joy and peace in believing, so that you may abound in hope by the power of the Holy Spirit" (Rom. 15:13). Let us then, as adults in the child's world, so saturate ourselves with hope that it will pour out of us like living water on a parched ground, nourishing the souls of the children in our midst. Let us anchor our children in a sense of the sacredness of life so that they will be able to face the future with hope.

You will remember that we began this book with a story about small boats in a sudden storm. Our lives are often like those small boats on the sea of life. A fisherman's prayer says it all: "Dear God, be good to me. The sea is so wide and my boat is so small." It is during these storms of life that our faith must remain steadfast and our hope in God strong. Children observe how we handle the events that come our way and are quick to imitate our reactions to life, whether it is with faith and hope or with fear.

An elderly woman I once knew always sang when the burdens of life threatened to undo her. During times of frustration and fear her favorite hymn was "Stand by Me":

> When the storms of life are raging,
> Stand by me.
> When the storms of life are raging,
> Stand by me.
>
> When the world is tossing me,
> Like a ship upon the sea,
> Thou who rulest wind and water,
> Stand by me.

There is something extraordinarily comforting about those timeless words. To know that we have One to whom we can turn, One who is stronger than ourselves and who cares for us, especially in the storms of life, gives us the hope and courage to go on.

A Word to the Churches

Although I have said that the parent, grandparent, and other significant adults in the home should be the primary nurturers of the spiritual life of the child, I cannot ignore the vital role the church plays in this matter. Parents need to be a part of the community of faith and urgently need the supportive role of this faith community as they parent their children in matters of the spirit.

Marjorie Thompson has said, "The first task of the larger church with respect to its families is to give them a vision—a spiritual and theological vision—of who they are, what they are called to, and how their family life connects with the depths of their faith."[10] More than ever before in the history of the Christian church, this is a task that must not be ignored.

She continues by saying that "one of most serious tasks of the church at large is to help its member families to *be* the body of Christ within the home....Then, as particular expressions of the all-inclusive family of God, church families become redeeming communities and thus sacraments of God's grace."[11] This is our hope for all families—that they become redeeming communities and sacraments of God's grace.

The church can do many things to help in this process. As I have said earlier, the community of faith must become what the small towns and villages once were: a loving community of people who care for and nurture the body, mind, and souls of their children. Through instruction and example, through liturgy and ritual, through stories and symbols, adults in the family of faith should embrace the precious children in their midst.

The church can also provide, on an ongoing basis, the assistance that parents need in order for their families to become redeeming communities and sacraments of God's grace. The church may do this by initiating a six-week course on the spiritual disciplines for parents, or organizing small groups where parents might meet and share ideas and grow together. It might do this by providing childcare and by having a retreat for parents who desperately need some time for renewal of their souls. The church might train older adults to be mentors to younger parents. Pairing more experienced parents with less experienced ones could be an invaluable ministry, giving much needed support to those who are calling out for help.

The community of faith must also look at its comprehensive program to see if it is meeting the total needs of parents and children who are within its fellowship. Is after-school care needed to prevent children from being alone too long in the afternoon? Would a tutoring program help children who are having trouble in school? Many retired teachers could offer their services if this assistance is needed.

Are there enough intergenerational activities in the church, or is every program geared to separating the family according to age? Children need to have interaction with older adults and vice versa. Some of children's greatest learning is in the context of relationships; by just being in the presence of an older friend who loves them, learning takes place.

Another way in which older persons can get involved in the lives of children in their churches is by starting an "Adopt a Grandchild" program. This is a helpful program for children whose grandparents do not live near them and is also meaningful to grandparents whose grandchildren live far away. A variation of this program is to have a "Secret Grandparent." The grandparents are paired with a child and are encouraged to send anonymous notes, small gifts, and messages. At a designated time, perhaps at a party at the church, their names would be revealed to the child and they would then get acquainted.

Many churches pair an adult with a confirmand to be their "Friend in the Faith." As the child moves toward confirmation, the older friend can be helpful in so many ways: for example, answering questions, sharing their own faith story, spending some time with the child, and giving small but meaningful gifts that reflect the faith journey that the child is on.

One church told me recently about a new program that they have organized called "Grandparents' Camp." Only the grandchildren and grandparents are allowed to attend. This serves two purposes: it frees the parents so that they can have some time apart, and it provides a wonderful bonding experience between the grandparents and grandchildren. Memories are made and stored that will be remembered throughout the lifetime of the child.

Not only should churches assess their programs for the children in their congregations, they should also assess their programs for the children who live within the shadow of the church. What should the church do for these children? What is God calling the church to be and to do? One of the main missions of the church should be a strong focus on children's ministries, to care for "the least of these" in our midst.[12]

Conclusion

In the eighth chapter of Romans we read, "For all who are led by the Spirit of God are children of God....When we cry, 'Abba! Father!' it is that very Spirit bearing witness with our spirit that we are children of God, and if children, then heirs, heirs of God and joint heirs with Christ" (Rom. 8:14-17). We have a spiritual heritage that claims us as God's children. This heritage claims us and our children to be children of the promise.

As we live out our lives in our homes, in the daily ebb and flow of life, Christ's love becomes the guiding force—the energy that sets in motion everything that we do. Day in and day out we strive to be, by precept and example, what Christ would have us be. We love unconditionally, we forgive, we listen, we instruct, we guide, we nurture our children in the spiritual life so that they may claim their rightful heritage as God's children. We give them the roots that they need to sustain them in the storms of life and then when the time is right, we give them wings and let them go. We are empowered to do this knowing that the faithful One who has claimed our children and knows them by name will be with them throughout their lives.

In the back of the book are two promise statements. The first, "The Hannah Promise," is for parents; the second, "The Lois Promise," is for grandparents. After you review these, spend some time in prayer considering the conditions of these statements. Then as the Holy Spirit leads, I invite you to prayerfully and reverently sign the appropriate promise statement—"The Hannah Promise" if you are a parent or "The Lois Promise" if you are a grandparent (in some cases, you might want to sign both promises if you are a parent and a grandparent). Remove the promise from this book and place it in your Bible or on your prayer table, covenanting with God that with God's help you will fulfill its conditions. Review it from time to time, add to it as God leads, and renew occasionally your vow to God to keep its conditions.

I have a great passion for the children of our world, those within our circle of love and those who are not within anyone's circle of love. What a powerful force it would be to have parents and grandparents praying in great masses across the world for our children! Even fifteen minutes a day would make a great difference. John Wesley said, "God seldom gives the Spirit to God's people...if they do not pray for it on all occasions; not only once, but many times. God does nothing except in answer to prayer."[13] If this is true—that God does nothing except in answer to prayer—what a mighty force of prayer we as parents and grandparents could be! It would be difficult even to imagine the difference our prayers could make in the lives of our children and grandchildren if we promised to pray faithfully for them fifteen minutes a day.

Rufus M. Jones has said, "You cannot command or compel people into holiness, you cannot increase their spiritual stature one cubit by any kind of force or compulsion. You can do it only by sharing your life with them, by making them feel your goodness, by your love and sacrifice for them."[14] By sharing our lives with our children, by living with them in unconditional love, by modeling for them the life of faith, and by praying for them constantly, we can make a difference in our children's lives. As parents and grandparents, let us all, as children of the promise, join in this sacred task of becoming spiritual guides to our precious children, knowing that the God who called us to this task will enable us for this holy pilgrimage.

Questions for Discussion

Introduction

1. Do you believe that the morality of a society is related to the spirituality of the people? Give examples, if possible.

2. In your opinion, are the moral and social foundations of institutions in our society cracking, as Amitai Etzioni stated? What causes you to think this?

3. What three things could you do to help alleviate the "threadbare texture of community" in which many children today live out their lives?

Chapter One

1. In what ways have God's promises been a force in your life? Which terminology do you like better—God's covenants or God's promises? Why?

2. Have you ever been tempted to try to leave your children "a blank slate" so that they could decide on their own beliefs at the proper time? If yes, what changed your mind? If no, on what grounds did you make that decision?

3. What are two spiritual disciplines that you could embrace that would enable you to live more fully in and embrace "the sacrament of the present moment"?

4. Read John 15:1-17. How does Jesus' parable of the vine and branches connect with your own sense of rootedness in the faith? How does this parable compare to the scenario of the lily pads, which are anchored by an unseen force? At this present moment in the life of your family, is it more like the small boats adrift in a storm or like the lily pads anchored securely by a stronger entity?

Chapter Two

1. What are the forces in society that prevent your family from being the spiritual unit you want it to be? What can you do about it?

2. In what ways do you need to nurture your own spiritual life so you can better nurture the spiritual life of your child?

3. Choose two of the spiritual disciplines outlined in this chapter and implement them in your life for one month. Record in your journal (just a small spiral notebook will do) what difference, if any, this has made in your life.

4. How can you, in your own family, prioritize and re-order your values so that you are able to live in the world but are not controlled or consumed by the values of the world?

5. Spend some time writing a promise statement for your family. Consider the following issues: What are your values? What is your faith system? What do you want to pass on to your children?

Chapter Three

1. In what ways are you already a spiritual guide to your children?

2. In what ways can you begin now to better guide the spirit of your child?

3. With which biblical example outlined in this chapter do you most closely identify? Which biblical example challenges you to grow beyond your present comfort zone?

4. Think about each special child in your life. As you do so, make a spiritual assessment of each one, listing the spiritual needs that you perceive in his or her life. Make a promise to God to pray daily for these spiritual needs.

Chapter Four

1. Chapter 4 names five major roles that grandparents fulfill today. Out of your life experiences, what other roles would you like to add to this list?

2. What is your greatest strength as a grandparent?

3. What do you need to do to improve your skills in being a spiritual guide to your grandchildren?

4. Name two special ways that you are nurturing the spirituality of your grandchild?

Chapter Five

1. What wisdom do you need from God to enable you to be a spiritual guide for your children or grandchildren?

2. What wisdom have you gained from the information that these parents and grandparents have shared?

3. Read Luke 2:52. What are specific ways that you can encourage your children to grow in "wisdom and in years, and in divine and human favor"?

4. Do you identify with the story *The Missing Piece*? How can we as Christians accept imperfections, troubles, and sorrows as a normal part of life and yet live daily a life that exemplifies joy and hope found in Christ?

Chapter Six

1. Read Luke 18:15-17; Matthew 18:1-3; Mark 9: 36-37; and Matthew 11:25. What can we learn from reading Jesus' interactions and statements about children?

2. In what ways have children been a spiritual guide to you? What can you learn from them in these experiences?

3. How can you better model hope in the future for children?

4. What can you do to help your church better meet the needs of children and their families?

Notes

Introduction

1. David Hay with Rebecca Nye, *The Spirit of the Child* (London: Fount, 1998), 160.

2. Ibid., 36.

3. Ibid., 18.

4. Ibid., 17.

5. Ibid., v.

6. Ibid., 17.

7. Amitai Etzioni, in the preface to the 1995 British edition of *The Spirit of Community*, quoted in Hay, 37.

8. Ibid.

Chapter One

1. "Mom on Motherhood," *Scholastic Parent and Child* (October/November 1997): 13.

2. Lewis Joseph Sherrill, *The Struggle of the Soul* (New York: Macmillan, 1963), 14–19.

3. Ibid., 18.

4. Debra G. Ball-Kilbourne, *Living as Covenant People* (Nashville, Tenn.: Cokesbury, 1992), 4.

5. David Lowes Watson, *Covenant Discipleship* (Nashville, Tenn.: Discipleship Resources, 1991), 113.

6. David Alexander and Pat Alexander, eds., *Eerdman's Handbook to the Bible* (Tring, England: Lion Publishing, 1973), 123–124.

7. Jean-Pierre de Caussade, *Abandonment to Divine Providence*, trans. John Beevers (New York: Doubleday, 1975), 20, 42.

8. I heard this concept first used by Gwen White, spiritual director and retreat leader.

9. Sofia Cavalletti et al., *The Good Shepherd and the Child* (New Rochelle, N.Y.: Don Bosco Multimedia, 1994), 11.

Chapter Two

1. Joseph P. Horrigan, M.D., Assistant Professor, Division of Child and Adolescent Psychiatry, Department of Psychiatry, University of North Carolina, interview by author, Chapel Hill, N.C., 10 June 1998.

2. Peter L. Benson and Carolyn H. Eklin, *Effective Christian Education: A National Study of Protestant Congregations* (Minneapolis: Search Institute, 1990), 4.

3. Margaret Guenther, *Holy Listening: The Art of Spiritual Direction* (Boston: Cowley Publications, 1992), 30.

4. Ibid., 1.

5. Kenneth Leech, *Soul Friend: An Invitation to Spiritual Direction* (San Francisco: HarperSanFrancisco, 1992), 193.

6. Sandra Schneiders, "The Contemporary Ministry of Spiritual Direction," Kevin G. Culligan, ed. *Spiritual Direction, Contemporary Readings* (Locust Valley, N.Y.: Living Flame Press, 1983), 46.

7. Richard J. Foster, *Celebration of Discipline: The Path to Spiritual Growth* (San Francisco: HarperSanFrancisco, 1978), 160.

8. Betty Shannon Cloyd, *Children and Prayer: A Shared Pilgrimage* (Nashville, Tenn.: Upper Room Books, 1997), 13.

9. Gerald May, *Care of Mind, Care of Spirit: A Psychiatrist Explores Spiritual Direction* (San Francisco: HarperSanFrancisco, 1982), 8.

10. Ibid.

11. Tilden Edwards, *Spiritual Friend: Reclaiming the Gift of Spiritual Direction* (New York: Paulist Press, 1980), 128–129.

12. John Dalrymple, *Simple Prayer*, quoted in Richard Foster, *Prayer: Finding the Heart's True Home* (San Francisco: HarperSanFranscisco, 1992), 74.

13. See Rueben P. Job and Norman Shawchuck, *A Guide to Prayer for all God's People* (Nashville, Tenn.: Upper Room Books, 1990).

14. Susan Shaughnessy, *Walking on Alligators*, quoted in Joyce Rupp, *Dear Heart, Come Home* (New York: The Crossroad Publishing Co., 1996), 11.

15. Marjorie J. Thompson, *Soul Feast: An Invitation to the Christian Spiritual Life* (Louisville, Ky.: Westminster John Knox Press, 1995), 103.

16. Bernard of Clairvaux, *Selections from the Writings of Bernard of Clairvaux*, ed. Douglas V. Steere (Nashville, Tenn.: The Upper Room, 1961), 28.

17. Francis of Assisi, *Selections from the Writings of St. Francis of Assisi*, ed. J. Minton Batten (Nashville, Tenn.: The Upper Room, 1952), 25.

18. Watson, *Covenant Discipleship*, 36.

19. *Ibid.,* 39, 64.

20. Foster, *Celebration of Discipline*, 6.

21. Polly Berrien Berends, *Whole Child/Whole Parent*, (New York: HarperCollins, 1997), 89.

Chapter Three

1. Hay, *The Spirit of the Child*, 145.

2. Gote Klingberg, "A Study of Religious Experience in Children from 9 to 13 Years of Age," *Religious Education* 54, no. 3 (May–June 1959): 211.

3. Hay, *The Spirit of the Child*, 137.

4. John Westerhoff III, *Bringing Up Children in the Christian Faith* (Minneapolis: Winston Press, 1980), 49.

5. *The New Interpreter's Bible*, vol. 9 (Nashville, Tenn: Abingdon Press, 1995), 703.

6. Guenther, *Holy Listening: The Art of Spiritual Direction*, 30.

7. Merton P. Strommen and A. Irene Strommen, *Five Cries of Parents* (San Francisco: Harper and Row, 1985), 153–157.

8. Hay, *The Spirit of the Child*,172.

9. Barbara Kymes Myers, *Young Children and Spirituality* (New York: Routledge, 1997), 63–64.

10. Hay, *The Spirit of the Child*, 163.

11. Gertrud Mueller Nelson, *To Dance with God* (New York: Paulist Press, 1986), 25.

12. Lecture by Dr. Charles R. Foster, Interim Dean and Professor of Religion and Education, Candler School of Theology, Atlanta, Ga., at Scarritt Bennett Center, Nashville, Tenn., June 27, 1998.

13. David Lowes Watson, "Bind Us Together," *The Interpreter* (January 1988): 24.

14. Francis W. Boelter, *The Covenant People of God* (Nashville, Tenn.: Tidings, 1971), 18.

15. Polly Berrien Berends, "Growing Together While Growing Separately," *Spirituality and Health* (Fall 1998): 32.

16. Story told by JoAnn Miller.

17. Guenther, *Holy Listening*, 118.

18. Ibid., 119.

19. Julian of Norwich, *Showings*, trans. Edmund Colledge and James Walsh (New York: Paulist Press, 1978), 225.

20. Berends, "Growing Together While Growing Separately," 32–33.

21. Betty Shannon Cloyd, *Children and Prayer: A Shared Pilgrimage* (Nashville, Tenn.: Upper Room Books, 1997), 24.

22. For an excellent resource for children on journaling, see Janet R. Knight and Lynn W. Gilliam, *My Journal: A Place to Write About God and Me* (Nashville, Tenn.: Upper Room Books, 1997).

23. Mary Pipher, *The Shelter of Each Other: Rebuilding Our Families* (New York: Ballantine Books, 1996), 145–149.

24. Betty Shannon Cloyd, "Teaching Children to Pray: A Sacred Trust," *Children's Teacher* (summer 1998): 3.

Chapter Four

1. Interview with Dr. Joseph P. Horrigan.

2. Charles E. Whalen Jr., foreword to *Connecting the Generations: Grandparenting for the New Millennium* by Roma Hanks (Gainesville, Ga.: The Warren Featherbone Foundation, 1998), ii.

3. Interview with Dr. Joseph P. Horrigan.

4. John Westerhoff III, *Bringing Up Children in the Christian Faith*, 16.

5. Story told to me by the Reverend Dr. Peter van Eys, pastor, Calvary United Methodist Church, Nashville, Tenn.

6. Howard Rice, *The Pastor as Spiritual Guide* (Nashville, Tenn.: Upper Room Books, 1998), 58.

7. Arthur Kornhaber, M.D., with Sondra Forsyth, *Grandparent Power!* (New York: Crown Publishers, Inc., 1994), 150.

8. Alan Jones in Guenther, *Holy Listening*, xii.

9. Story told by Margaret Freeman, mother of Laura Freeman.

Chapter Five

1. Interview with Dr. Joseph P. Horrigan.

2. Ibid.

3. Ibid.

4. Ibid.

5. Ibid.

6. Ibid.

7. Shel Silverstein, *The Missing Piece* (New York: HarperCollins, 1976).

8. *The Confessions of St. Augustine*, trans. John K. Ryan (New York: Doubleday, 1960), 272.

Chapter Six

1. Marjorie J. Thompson, *Family the Forming Center: A Vision of the Role of Family in Spiritual Formation* (Nashville, Tenn.: Upper Room Books, 1996), 70.

2. Jerome W. Berryman, *Godly Play* (San Francisco: HarperSanFrancisco, 1991. Minneapolis: Augsburg Fortress, 1995), 148–149.

3. *The Daily Wesley*, ed. Donald E. Demaray (Anderson, Ind.: Briston House, 1994), 378.

4. Thompson, *Family the Forming Center*, 70.

5. Ibid.

6. Frederic Brussat and Mary Ann Brussat, *Spiritual Literacy: Reading the Sacred in Everyday Life* (New York: Scribner, 1996), 194.

7. Rubem A. Alves, quoted in Brussat, *Spiritual Literacy*, 195.

8. Augustine, *The Wisdom of Saint Augustine*, comp. David Winter (Grand Rapids, Mich.: William B. Eerdmans Publishing Co., 1997), 8.

9. Ronald S. James, "Looking at Power," *Weavings: A Journal of the Christian Spiritual Life* (May/June 1999): 9.

10. Thompson, *Family the Forming Center*, 143.

11. Ibid., 144.

12. For excellent information on how to become a church that is truly meeting the needs of children see the Bishops Initiative on Children and Poverty entitled *A Church for All God's Children*. It is available through The General Board of Church and Society, The

General Board of Discipleship, The General Board of Global Min-
istries, and the General Board of Higher Education and Ministry.
Another good resource is *Putting Children and Their Families First: A
Planning Handbook for Congregations* by Laura Dean Ford Friedrich,
General Board of Global Ministries, 475 Riverside Drive, New York,
NY 10115.

13. *The Daily Wesley*, 360.

14. Rufus Jones, *The Double Search*, quoted in Rueben P. Job and
Norman Shawchuck, *A Guide to Prayer for All God's People* (Nashville,
Tenn.: Upper Room Books, 1990), 187.

Bibliography

Alexander, David, and Pat Alexander, eds. *Eerdmans' Handbook to the Bible.* Tring, England: Lion Publishing, 1973.

Augustine. *The Confessions of St. Augustine.* Trans. John K. Ryan. New York: Doubleday, 1960.

_____. *The Wisdom of St. Augustine.* Comp. David Winter. Grand Rapids, Mich.: William B. Eerdman's Publishing Co., 1997.

Ball-Kilbourne, Debra G. *Living as Covenant People.* Nashville, Tenn.: Cokesbury, 1992.

Benson, Peter L., and Carolyn H. Eklin. *Effective Christian Education: A National Study of Protestant Congregations.* Minneapolis: Search Institute, 1990.

Berends, Polly Berrien. "Growing Together While Growing Separately," *Spirituality and Health* (fall 1998): 32–33.

_____. *Whole Child/Whole Parent.* New York: HarperCollins, 1997.

Bernard of Clairvaux. *Selections from the Writings of Bernard of Clairvaux.* Ed. Douglas V. Steere. Nashville, Tenn.: The Upper Room, 1961.

Berryman, Jerome W. *Godly Play.* San Francisco: HarperSanFrancisco, 1991; Minneapolis: Augsburg Fortress, 1995.

Boelter, Francis W. *The Covenant People of God.* Nashville, Tenn.: Tidings, 1971.

Brussat, Frederic, and Mary Ann Brussat. *Spiritual Literacy: Reading the Sacred in Everyday Life.* New York: Scribner, 1996.

Caussade, Jean-Pierre de. *Abandonment to Divine Providence.* Trans. John Beevers. New York: Doubleday, 1975.

Cavalletti, Sofia, Patricia Coulter, Gianna Gobbi, and Silvana Q. Montanaro, M.D. *The Good Shepherd and the Child.* New Rochelle, N.Y.: Don Bosco Multimedia, 1994.

Cloyd, Betty Shannon. *Children and Prayer: A Shared Pilgrimage.* Nashville, Tenn.: Upper Room Books, 1997.

_____. "Teaching Children to Pray: A Sacred Trust," *Children's Teacher* (summer 1998): 3.

Culligan, Kevin, ed. *Spiritual Direction, Contemporary Readings.* Locust Valley, N.Y.: Living Flame Press, 1983.

The Daily Wesley: Excerpts for Every Day in the Year. Ed. Donald E. Demaray. Anderson, Ind.: Briston House, Ltd., 1994.

Edwards, Tilden. *Spiritual Friend: Reclaiming the Gift of Spiritual Direction.* New York: Paulist Press, 1980.

Foster, Richard J. *Celebration of Discipline: The Path to Spiritual Growth.* San Francisco: HarperSanFrancisco, 1978.

_____. *Prayer: Finding the Heart's True Home.* San Francisco: HarperSanFrancisco, 1992.

Francis of Assisi. *Selections from the Writings of St. Francis of Assisi.* Ed. J. Minton Batten. Nashville, Tenn.: The Upper Room, 1952.

Guenther, Margaret. *Holy Listening: The Art of Spiritual Direction.* Boston: Cowley Publications, 1992.

Hanks, Roma. *Connecting the Generations: Grandparenting for the New Millennium.* Gainesville, Ga.: Warren Featherbone Foundation, 1998.

Hay, David, with Rebecca Nye. *The Spirit of the Child.* London: Fount, 1998.

James, Ronald S. "Looking at Power," *Weavings: A Journal of the Christian Spiritual Life* (May/June 1999): 6–13.

Job, Rueben P., and Norman Shawchuck. *A Guide to Prayer for All God's People.* Nashville, Tenn.: Upper Room Books, 1990.

Julian of Norwich. *Showings.* Trans. Edmund Colledge and James Walsh. New York: Paulist Press, 1978.

Knight, Janet R., and Lynn W. Gilliam. *My Journal: A Place to Write About God and Me.* Nashville, Tenn.: Upper Room Books, 1997.

Kornhaber, Arthur, M.D., with Sondra Forsyth. *Grandparent Power!* New York: Crown Publishers, Inc., 1994.

Leech, Kenneth. *Soul Friend: An Invitation to Spiritual Direction.* San Francisco: HarperSanFrancisco, 1992.

May, Gerald. *Care of Mind, Care of Spirit: A Psychiatrist Explores Spiritual Direction.* San Francisco: HarperSanFrancisco, 1982.

Nelson, Gertrud Mueller. *To Dance with God.* New York: Paulist Press, 1986.

Persky, Margaret McMillan. *Living in God's Time: A Parent's Guide to Nurturing Children Throughout the Christian Year.* Nashville, Tenn.: Upper Room Books, 1999.

Pipher, Mary, *The Shelter of Each Other: Rebuilding Our Families*. New York: Ballantine Books, 1996.

Rice, Howard. *The Pastor as Spiritual Guide*. Nashville, Tenn.: Upper Room Books, 1998.

Rupp, Joyce. *Dear Heart, Come Home*. New York: The Crossroad Publishing Co., 1997.

Sherrill, Lewis Joseph. *The Struggle of the Soul*. New York: Macmillan, 1963.

Silverstein, Shel. *The Missing Piece*. New York: HarperCollins, 1976.

Strommen, Merton P., and A. Irene Strommen. *Five Cries of Parents*. San Francisco: Harper and Row, 1985.

Thompson, Marjorie J. *Family The Forming Center*. Nashville, Tenn.: Upper Room Books, 1996.

_____. *Soul Feast: An Invitation to the Christian Spiritual Life*. Louisville, Ky.: Westminster John Knox Press, 1995.

Watson, David Lowes. "Bind Us Together," *The Interpreter* (January 1988): 22–24.

_____. *Covenant Discipleship*. Nashville, Tenn.: Discipleship Resources, 1991.

Westerhoff, John H., III. *Bringing Up Children in the Christian Faith*. Minneapolis: Winston Press, 1980.

The Hannah Promise
(For Parents)

The Hannah Promise is based on the story of Hannah, who longed for a child (1 Samuel 1). Hannah promised God that if she had a son, she would give him to the Lord. When God blessed her with a son, she named him Samuel. After he was weaned, Hannah remembered her promise and brought Samuel to Eli at the Temple and left him there saying, "As long as he lives, he is given to the Lord."

I accept the Hannah Promise, and with God's help, I will:

1. Pray at least fifteen minutes a day for my children.

2. Bring my children into God's presence by teaching them to pray and by taking them to God's house as often as possible.

3. Recognize that all children (my own and the children of the world) are gifts from God and are our greatest treasure. Honoring this fact, I will order my life in such a way as to provide the proper emotional, physical, mental, and spiritual nurture for my own children and will honestly endeavor, with God's help, to reach out to provide this nurture to at least one child who is not receiving it.

Signed _____

Date _____

From *Parents and Grandparents as Spiritual Guides: Nurturing Children of the Promise* by Betty Shannon Cloyd. Nashville, Tenn.: Upper Room Books, 2000.

I have signed the Hannah Promise. I mail this card as a symbol of my commitment to nurture the spiritual lives of children.

The Hannah Promise

_____
Name

_____
Address

_____
City/State/Zip

_____
E-mail Address

❏ Please send me information about additional family resources.

The Hannah Promise

_____
Name

_____
Address

_____
City/State/Zip

_____
E-mail Address

❏ Please send me information about additional family resources.

Preparing the Way
  for the Emerging Generation

NO POSTAGE
NECESSARY
IF MAILED
IN THE
UNITED STATES

BUSINESS REPLY MAIL
FIRST-CLASS MAIL PERMIT NO. 1540 NASHVILLE TN

POSTAGE WILL BE PAID BY ADDRESSEE

UPPER
ROOM.
MINISTRIES

THE HANNAH PROMISE
PO BOX 340012
NASHVILLE, TN 37203-9540

The Lois Promise
(For Grandparents)

The Lois Promise is based on 2 Timothy 1:5. Paul writes to Timothy, "I am reminded of your sincere faith, a faith that lived first in your grandmother Lois and your mother Eunice and now, I am sure, lives in you."

I accept the Lois Promise, and with God's help, I will:

1. Pray at least fifteen minutes a day for my grandchildren.

2. Endeavor through scripture, prayer, stories, and example to pass my faith on to my grandchildren.

3. Recognize that all children (my own grandchildren and the children of the world) are gifts from God and are our greatest treasure. Honoring this fact, I will order my life in such a way as to provide the proper emotional, physical, mental, and spiritual nurture for my own grandchildren and will honestly endeavor, with God's help, to reach out to provide this nurture to at least one child who is not receiving it.

Signed _____

Date _____

From *Parents and Grandparents as Spiritual Guides: Nurturing Children of the Promise* by Betty Shannon Cloyd. Nashville, Tenn.: Upper Room Books, 2000.

I have signed the Lois Promise. I mail this card as a symbol of my commitment to nurture the spiritual lives of my grandchildren as well as the spiritual lives of other children I meet.

The Lois Promise

Name

Address

City/State/Zip

E-mail Address

❑ Please send me information about additional family resources.

The Lois Promise

Name

Address

City/State/Zip

E-mail Address

❑ Please send me information about additional family resources.

Preparing the Way
   for the Emerging Generation

BUSINESS REPLY MAIL
FIRST-CLASS MAIL PERMIT NO. 1540 NASHVILLE TN

POSTAGE WILL BE PAID BY ADDRESSEE

UPPER
ROOM.
MINISTRIES

THE LOIS PROMISE
PO BOX 340012
NASHVILLE, TN 37203-9540

||..||.|....|..|.|.|||....||.|.|..|.|..|.|.|||..|...||

Preparing the Way
   for the Emerging Generation

NO POSTAGE
NECESSARY
IF MAILED
IN THE
UNITED STATES

BUSINESS REPLY MAIL
FIRST-CLASS MAIL PERMIT NO. 1540 NASHVILLE TN

POSTAGE WILL BE PAID BY ADDRESSEE

UPPER
ROOM.
MINISTRIES

THE LOIS PROMISE
PO BOX 340012
NASHVILLE, TN 37203-9540

||..||.|....|..|.|.|||....||.|.|..|.|..|.|.|||..|...||